THE FLAVOR OF
SMALL-TOWN AMERICA

This compendium of uniquely delicious family recipes from the personal collection of "Miss Mary" Bobo celebrates the down-home cooking and heartwarming hospitality of Lynchburg, Tennessee. Here you will find tried-and-true recipes for such traditional favorites as Skillet Corn Bread . . . Country Fried Steak with Buttermilk Gravy . . . Candied Sweet Potatoes . . . fresh and luscious Peach Cobbler . . . and dozens more hearty and satisfying dishes that are as welcome at small family suppers as they are at large holiday get-togethers.

Miss Mary's
DOWN-HOME
COOKING

"A WONDERFUL BOOK . . . Makes entertaining easy, creative, and delicious."—TAMPA NEWS-CHIEF

"A source of fine food and a link to a bygone America. . . . Takes a nostalgic look at small-town America and the robust diet of Tennessee."—NEW HAVEN REGISTER

DIANA DALSASS is also the author of *The Good Cake Book* (Plume) and *Cashews, Lentils, Apples and Oats*.

MISS MARY'S
BOARDINGHOUSE

Miss Mary's Down-Home COOKING

Recipes from Small-Town America

by Diana Dalsass

A Main Street Book

10 9 8 7 6 5 4 3 2 1

Published by Sterling Publishing Co., Inc.
387 Park Avenue South, New York, NY 10016
© 1984 by Diana Dalsass
© 2002 by Sterling Publishing Co., Inc.
Distributed in Canada by Sterling Publishing
c/o Canadian Manda Group, One Atlantic Avenue, Suite 105
Toronto, Ontario, Canada M6K 3E7
Distributed in Great Britain by Chrysalis Books
64 Brewery Road, London N7 9NT, England
Distributed in Australia by Capricorn Link (Australia) Pty. Ltd.
P.O. Box 704, Windsor, NSW 2756, Australia

Manufactured in China

Sterling ISBN 1-4027-0148-9

To Mary Bobo
1 8 8 1 – 1 9 8 3
whose life goes on in the recipes
of this book

Acknowledgments

I would like to gratefully thank Lynne Tolley, a native of Lynchburg, for the help she has provided in obtaining recipes from the cooks at the Bobo House. Lynne has also been a valuable source of information about the food lore of the area, as well as about the boardinghouse and Miss Mary herself. Following the death of Mary Bobo in 1983, Lynne has become the proprietress of the Bobo House.

I would also like to extend my appreciation to the several Bobo House cooks, who so willingly provided me with Miss Mary's special recipes. These include Helen Daniel, Louise Gregory, Barbara Ruth McGowen, and Leola Dismukes, who was a cook at the boardinghouse for fifteen years until she retired.

And finally, I would like to acknowledge the help and background information provided by the folks at the Jack Daniel Distillery, as well as the many residents of the town, who so patiently answered all my questions about their lives.

Contents

MOORE COUNTY COURTHOUSE

MISS MARY'S
BOARDINGHOUSE

COUNTY JAIL

LYNCHBURG
TENNESSEE

Introduction

THIS BOOK is more than just a collection of recipes. Rather, it's a portrayal of a way of life that is almost extinct in most parts of the country. Today it is rare to find a town that has hardly changed since the turn of the century, or one where the majority of its citizens are born, raised, and grow old within its boundaries.

Lynchburg, Tennessee, is just such a place. With an "official" population of 361, it is the seat of Moore County, the largest town in the smallest county in Tennessee. An area where the Tennessee Bluegrass meets the Cumberland Mountains, this is farming country. The land is verdant, providing good grazing for fine cattle and dairy herds. Hogs, mules, chickens, and even hound dogs are raised here.

While the outer boundaries of Lynchburg stretch for miles across the lush farmland, the actual town is still close to the size it always was—about a single square block. For anyone driving by on Highway 55, Lynchburg was easy to miss until the townsfolk installed their only traffic light—done not so much to make the town more noticeable but to protect departing visitors. The traffic light ensures that anyone turning onto the highway from the town doesn't get hit by one of the few on-coming cars that might come speeding by.

Today the Lynchburg town square looks pretty much as it did around the turn of the century. Most of the buildings are un-changed. The Moore County Courthouse, an impressive red brick structure built in 1884, dominates the square. The nearby jail is even older than the courthouse. The potted geraniums on its front porch give the building almost a cozy look, even though it has had very few inmates to admire them over the years.

The stores of Lynchburg are as much fun for browsing and passing time as they ever were. The Lynchburg Hardware Store has always been a place for the town's men to gather and get caught up on the local news or discuss politics, sports, and crops. They sit for hours by the big pot-bellied stove in the back of the store, playing checkers and swapping stories. Out front there's sure to be at least one old-timer whittling on a piece of hardwood. No one as ever been able to categorize exactly what this store sells. It carries, in addition to the handbook of country lore entitled *On Man and the Good Life* by former local writer and farmer Emmett Gowen,* various basic hardware items and farm equipment, a few old-fashioned iron pots and pans for the kitchen, "hogwashers" (overalls) and other clothes, and then some items that just somehow arrived there—like the "secondhand" coffin that one family decided not to keep after a dying relative ordered two models so he could choose the one he wanted.

The women of the town get together to exchange news in the Ladies Handicraft Shop. The store sells only handmade items, like doll clothes, baby booties and bibs, quilts, embroidered place-mats and napkins, floppy stuffed animals, handpainted note cards, and the like. When an item is sold, the person who made it receives ninety percent of the sale price; the rest goes toward the running expenses of the store. All the women who sell their wares in the store must donate two days' time per month as saleswomen. However, this is no chore; each woman looks forward to her turn as an opportunity to sit and chat for hours with friends who drop by.

* Excerpts from it appear throughout the present book.

The White Rabbit Saloon—which hasn't been a saloon since 1909, when Moore County went dry—now offers a good lunch at a fair price, and the Soda Shop still serves real old-fashioned sodas at the original marble soda fountain counter.

But to describe Lynchburg only as a peaceful small town would be to omit what is unique about this special spot in south-central Tennessee and what attracts thousands of visitors each year—and that is the Jack Daniel Distillery. Registered in 1866, it is the oldest distillery in the United States and has been placed on the National Register of Historic Places.

Lynchburg could be called a "company town," but not in the sense that employees have to adhere to strict rules of social behavior or entertain the boss to get ahead, or have the "right" wife or belong to a country club. Lynchburg is a company town because most of the townsfolk work for the distillery, doing jobs they're proud of. The distillery is the lifeblood of Lynchburg—and that's just fine with the people who live there.

The inhabitants of Lynchburg, mostly descendants of Scottish and English pioneers, are a self-sufficient lot. For the past two centuries, they've produced their own music and dance. In fact, it has only been since the relatively recent arrival of television that the community has given up speaking the Elizabethan English that was kept alive for generations in this isolated pocket of America. These people are content to live in the ways of their ancestors; they feel life has been good to them, so they're not interested in running off to the nearest big city to seek fame and fortune. People here are proud to follow in the footsteps of their parents.

One example of the enormous self-sufficiency of the townsfolk is the way in which they survived the Great Depression. Those born too late to have lived through that period of hardship have heard stories from their parents and grandparents about what life was like then. While in most parts of the country people now tend to lose contact with their elders and therefore with that part of their past, in Lynchburg the majority of people stay put, and so, through family stories, their relatives' remembrances become their own history.

The people of Lynchburg were able to adjust to the Depression because long before it actually happened they had already experienced massive unemployment when Prohibition all but closed the Jack Daniel Distillery for more than a decade, starting in 1920. During that time only a small quantity of its Tennessee whiskey was made, to be sold by prescription "for medicinal purposes only." (In the Jack Daniel's archives, a few old bottles produced in the Twenties bear that phrase on the label.)

Because most of the men and many of the women in Lynchburg were employees of the distillery, these people had to find other means of making a living long before the Depression. While some folks faced with the same situation might have moved off to the nearest big city, people in Lynchburg felt too great a sense of community to leave, and so the lush farmland that had previously supported the few cows, hogs, and chickens that each family raised for personal consumption now became their sole means of livelihood. People started growing wheat, corn, tobacco, rye, and hay, and these crops, along with their gardens, permitted them to be almost totally self-sufficient. As one old farmer said: "We raised everything we needed except sugar. There was even a mill to grind our wheat into flour and our corn into meal." They killed their own hogs, cured their own hams and bacon, and rendered their own lard.

Jack Daniel's nephew, Lem Motlow, who inherited the distillery after his uncle's death, turned to raising mules, and when he had an ample number of these animals, he distributed a poster advertising the "final letting" (or auctioning off) of 3,000 mules to railroad construction companies, mining and drilling concerns, military forts and posts, prospectors, farmers, and trail outfitters, all of whom had use for mules in their work. The mules were classified according to type, from plow mules (minimum $75 per head), extra-heavy-duty mules (minimum $200 per head), to pack and riding mules (minimum $130 per head). Two stock trains with parlor accommodations for buyers departed daily from nearby Tullahoma station for "Nashville, Chicago, The Gold Mines and points West."

Thus, when the Depression came, producing such devastating effects elsewhere, life in Lynchburg went on much as it had in the previous decade, except that money got a whole lot scarcer. One Lynchburg resident recalls that the "cream check" was her family's only income. Another remembers that they were lucky to sell their wheat for 50 cents a bushel. As for cattle, young calves were purchased for 2¼ *cents* per pound; a year later, after they had been fattened up and were ready to be sold for beef, the cattle brought only 2½ cents a pound.

Although life was hard during those years, the way in which people in Lynchburg banded together to help one another out eased the strain. When it came to harvesting the wheat, for example, the town's only threshing machine was sent from farm to farm, with a day allotted to each place to bring in the harvest. On the day that the thresher was at a given farm about thirty farmers took turns helping out, and all the wives joined forces to provide a hearty noon-day meal for their menfolk. Roast chicken, roast beef, chicken pies, potatoes, beans, biscuits, and apple pie were served outside, picnic-style, to the hungry men.

Tiring as it was both for the men bringing in the wheat and for the women cooking in such prodigious quantities day after day, it was work of this sort that formed a major part of the social life of the town. Lynchburg did not have then and does not have now such recreations as movie theaters, elegant restaurants, or country clubs. Visiting the sick, helping out when help was needed, and church work made up the fabric of the town's social life. These were the accepted ways of socializing, for day-to-day living was so filled with household and farm chores that people simply couldn't afford the time to get together otherwise.

One of the greatest of all social gatherings—even though it usually came as a result of a calamity—was the quilting bee. From time to time, when a house burned down, all the women in the town would gather to make quilts for the disaster victims' new home. Generally twelve women worked on a single quilt, with six new quilts being sewn at once, each spread out in a different room of the home of the woman holding the bee. Each of the seventy-two women brought a covered dish with her; the lunch was a happy event, one of the few times that so many good friends had the opportunity to get together. By the end of the day, despite pauses for chatter and gossip, six splendid new quilts would have been completed for the needy family. Not all quilting bees came in the wake of a misfortune. An upcoming wedding was another occasion that warranted a quilting bee. These quilts—heirlooms now—were the town's gift to the new couple.

A diary, written by a Lynchburg woman named Sue Dance Record in 1896, and excerpted throughout this book, presents a clear picture of the everyday chores as well as the social life of the town. Although the entries record the true hardships and sorrows of the time, especially when friends fell ill and there was little that could be done but offer comfort, they also convey the many very real satisfactions and rewards that a homier life can bring to those open to accept and appreciate them.

Today the social life of Lynchburg isn't very different from that of almost a century ago. Certainly, there are fewer calamities and life is easier, but residents are quick to point out that, even so, little has changed. Although they don't have to clean kerosene lamps, as they did in the old days, and they now have central heating instead of wood stoves, the way of life is amazingly similar to that of their parents and grandparents. Sunday afternoons are still reserved for visiting friends and relatives, and the old and sick are visited daily by their friends. The church remains the center of most organized activities; spaghetti suppers and bake sales are still the traditional way of raising money to refurbish the church kitchen or pay for new prayer books. As one woman remarked, "We are blessed with just so many things to do in this itty-bitty town."

It goes without saying that when there are so few people in a town everyone knows everyone else. In fact, most Lynchburg residents can count a couple of dozen or more relatives who live "just down the road a ways," or "up over the next hill." But even when every face in a town is almost as familiar as every other, there are always a few people who stand out and are especially significant. These are the people who seem to hold the town together, who are the first that come to mind when any social gathering is planned, people whom the townsfolk admire, respect, and depend on. Until she died in 1983, just shy of her 102nd birthday, Mrs. Mary Bobo, who ran the boardinghouse in Lynchburg, was one of these people.

When "Miss Mary," as she was known in town, turned 100 on July 10, 1981, a special edition of the *Moore County News* was devoted to birthday greetings from her well-wishers, and the Mayor of Lynchburg, Bobby E. Murray, proclaimed the day Mary Bobo Day.

The memoirs that Miss Mary wrote for that day give a picture of her life and times in the corner of Tennessee that was her home for over a century.

I was born July 10, 1881 in Lynchburg, Tennessee. Later my father bought a large farm from Townsend Green. We moved to that farm, which had a nice two-story colonial home. We had several horses. We had mares and mules that worked and plowed and hitched to the wagon. We also had cattle and hogs.

We were planning to go to Florida when my father took sick and died. He was only thirty-nine years old. His children were all small.

My mother had tenants on the farm and so always managed to make a good living for us. She raised corn, wheat, rye, oats, etc. We took the wheat to the flour mill for bread. We took the corn to the mill for meal to make corn bread. It was also fed to the stock. We also had horses to ride and to pull the buggy. We also had a two-seated surrey, which is very rare and noticeable now. We milked the cows and churned the butter. I have milked a cow myself. We killed hogs for meat.

We had a large smoke house where the meat was cared for. We had a pump for water and a trough with cold water to keep the milk. We changed the water often. We cooked on wood stoves back then. We used iron skillets and deep pots for cooking, as well as tin pie pans. We used our own gardens for food. We bought sugar, coffee, soda and other extras.

My mother used to tell us when she was a little girl, during the Civil War, how they would hear soldiers tramping and run and hide. Being a rich agricultural district, it was constantly being preyed upon by foraging parties sent out from the Army stationed at near points. They had to live in constant fear of bushwhackers and raiding parties.

My mother was a good Christian woman. She took her children to Sunday School and Church. I am the oldest member now of that same church, Lynchburg Methodist.

School days were happy days. I first went to the old Academy, located above where the Jack Daniel Distillery is now. I was in chart class* there. I rode with my father on his yellow horse.

---

* Chart class came before the pupil received his or her first reader. The chart was something like a slate on which students learned their ABC's.

Later I went to the new school in Lynchburg. Ophelia, my sister, and I loved the piano. We rode to school in a buggy and put the horse in someone's barn. We took our lunch every day. This consisted of ham, sausage or chicken with biscuit and a pie or cake.

We wore calico, gingham or woolen dresses. We wore hoods or fascinators on our heads. We always wore pretty blue veils over our faces in winter. It really was cold weather then.

At the close of school, we had two days they called Examination Days. Parents all went and had dinner on the ground.* We had concerts with speeches, dialogues, piano solos and duets. Ophelia and I took music and had to do a lot of practicing.

In the summer, the teachers gave a two-week Institute with classes and programs. We went to that, too. Ophelia and I both had a part in the spelling match and both won on our side.

I then went to Winchester Normal for two years. . . . Later I married Lacy Jackson Bobo, who went by the name of Jack. He lived on the farm next to ours. After we married, we lived at his home for a while but later moved to Estill Springs, where he and my older half-brother went into business.

Mary Bobo had two children, five grandchildren, twelve great-grandchildren, and twelve great-great-grandchildren, which means that she was related by marriage to a whole lot of folks who live in Lynchburg, but apart from that fact and the extraordinary length of her very active life, Miss Mary made a major contribution to the heart and soul of the town.

In 1908 she and her husband opened their boardinghouse,

---

* A "dinner on the ground" is a local expression still in use. For example, the church might invite everyone to a "dinner on the ground." Although the food is usually laid out on tables, people eat on the ground on blankets.

and she soon became known for her fine cooking throughout Moore County, and later the State of Tennessee, and eventually to people all over the country.

She described the boardinghouse in her memoirs:

> Dr. E. Y. Salmon owned the property. He started practicing here in 1857. We bought it after he died. This has been a good home and I love it.

> There is a lot of history to this property. Thomas Roundtree was the original proprietor of the lands where Lynchburg is located. He built his log house on the lot where my home now stands. He laid out the town about the year 1818 and sold lots. There is a spring on my property and another spring under my house. We used to keep milk, butter, watermelons, etc. there.

> We started running a boardinghouse in 1908. It used to be called the "Bobo Hotel" until we took our sign down. So many people have stayed here over the years. We had government men that worked at the Distillery and we had lots of teachers, salesmen, etc. All of the rooms had two in a room.

The building that housed the Bobo Hotel, which was always more of a boardinghouse than a regular hotel, is conveniently located just about a block from the Lynchburg town square. It's a big, square wooden building, painted white, with graceful columns on either side of the generous front porch. A white picket fence surrounds the house, and "out back" there's a nice-sized vegetable garden.

A long time ago, there was also an icehouse next door, and Mary and Jack Bobo had a secondary business selling ice to the community. Huge blocks of ice were shipped from Tullahoma, over in the next county, and were preserved in sawdust. Customers came by to purchase a nickel or dime's worth, and Jack would chip off a chunk with his ice pick. Needless to say, the Bobos themselves went through plenty of ice, since iced tea containing lots of crushed ice was always served to guests at the noon meal.

Inside the house, there were four guest bedrooms upstairs, and another three downstairs, which took up most of that floor. Even the living room was converted to an extra bedroom. Thus, the main "living space" in the house was the large dining room, with its big table that seated twelve. A clean white tablecloth was always on the table, which was laid with white china and plain silverware. The dining room walls were decorated with country scenes painted by members of the family.

The Bobos lived simply. But "living simply" was not an easy task in those days. A wood stove was used for cooking, and additional stoves—one in each bedroom—supplied the heat (although Tennessee is part of the South, winters in the Lynchburg hills are about as cold and snowy as in parts of New England). Throughout the long winter all the stoves had to be fueled with hand-chopped wood. In summer, the wood stove in the kitchen made the room mighty hot. Only in recent years did the boardinghouse acquire an automatic dishwasher; before that, all dishes, pots, and pans were washed and dried by hand, and linens were washed on a big scrub board.

In the years when the Bobo Hotel functioned as a boardinghouse, the day began early. Miss Mary would be up at dawn, fixing a hearty breakfast for her boarders. Then, when the mood struck her, she would start making the yeast rolls for the noon meal. At nine o'clock, the cook arrived—often with a basketful of beans or peas that she had brought home the previous evening to snap or shell.

At noon, a bell would call all the diners in to eat. The midday meal was the main meal of the day. There were always about a dozen people sitting around the table. In addition to the Bobos and their boarders, there were often several unmarried men who worked in Lynchburg and who appreciated a good hot dinner. At the end of the day, supper was served—a meal similar to breakfast, consisting of scrambled eggs, ham, sausages, and grits.

The Bobo Hotel attracted a number of boarders, some of whom stayed as long as several years at a time. Only a few generations ago, it was considered improper for a young single woman to live on her own, so female teachers or home economists with the agricultural extension service who moved to Lynchburg welcomed the respectability of staying at Miss Mary's. Single men, too, often preferred living quarters where the cooking and cleaning were done by someone else.

In recent years, the boardinghouse underwent some changes, as Mary Bobo mentioned in her memoirs.

My husband, Jack, died May 27, 1948. I had lived alone up until age 98, when I fell and broke my hip. Now I have two nice ladies who take turns staying with me.

A few years ago, I started feeding Jack Daniel Distillery's invited guests and am not open to the public anymore. During the winter, we just use the upstairs rooms, but during the rest of the year we feed from fifty to a hundred people, five days a week. I stay out of the kitchen now. But up until age 98, I still ordered the groceries, planned the menus, wrote the checks, etc. I wonder how many more business people kept going at that age!

A number of stories about the boardinghouse—some probably exaggerated over the years—are still told by the townsfolk, who delight in their recollections of the odd people who came to stay at Mary Bobo's. They tell of the grocery store owner who was not only miserly but also so distrustful of banking his hard-earned cash that he hid it under his mattress instead. Every day when Mouse (Miss Mary's faithful servant, who remained with her for forty-four years) made the bed, he carefully tucked the blankets around the green bills, as if they weren't even there. Apparently, the grocer only spent money when he was intoxicated—something that rarely happened in Lynchburg. But on a visit to the Chicago World's Fair, he overindulged and returned with a brand-new Model T Ford. Since he didn't know how to drive, and wasn't about to learn, the new car was mounted on blocks in the Bobo garage, and there it remained.

Everyone who ate at Miss Mary's remembers the long-range feud between Tom Motlow, the banker, and Will Parks, who owned the Ford dealership in town. Tom was adamant on the subject of cars, claiming that everyone should either walk or ride a horse. When both men sat down to dine at the table, Tom would arouse the ire of Will by remarking that he had once again refused to lend money to some upstanding citizen who had requested a loan to purchase a Ford from Mr. Parks. The feud went on for so long that when Tom Motlow finally broke down and bought a car for himself, he chose a Chevrolet.

Among the more peculiar characters to board at Miss Mary's were the revenuers. Then, as now, the distillery had to pay a tax on its whiskey, but in earlier times, the government maintained a full-time employee in Lynchburg whose job it was to count the number of whiskey barrels that were emptied, in order to make certain that taxes were paid on each. In fact, the revenuer was the *only* man to hold the keys to the distillery's warehouses. (Even the company's owner did not have a set.)

The most difficult revenuer was a Mr. Moore, who enjoyed the exercise afforded by his back-and-forth walks between the boardinghouse and the distillery. The townsfolk, who were friendly even to strangers, kept stopping to offer him a ride. Finally, in frustration, the revenuer purchased a bicycle. When a wheel fell off shortly thereafter, rather than have it repaired, Mr. Moore pushed the bicycle on his walks, just so that no one would stop and offer him a ride.

Guests might come and go, but the tradition of good food at Miss Mary's was constant. Indeed, good food has always been important to the people of Lynchburg, and as far back as anyone can remember, cooking, baking, and the sharing of food accompanied every social occasion. Then and now, housewives vie to make the best cakes, to put up the best canned fruits, to make the lightest biscuits or the most flavorful gravies. And whenever a woman talks about how *she* makes a certain dish, she'll explain how she adds a bit more sugar or cooks it just a little bit longer, so that it turns out just a tiny bit better than the same dish made by any of her neighbors.

There's probably no area in which Lynchburg women try to excel more than in the foods they prepare for others. And there's probably also no other single aspect of their life that's still done in exactly the same way it was generations ago, for the execution of these recipes that are lovingly passed down from mother to daughter is carried out with an almost religious devotion to maintaining the standards of excellence set by their ancestors.

Back in the Depression, Lynchburg women formed a bridge club that is still in existence today. Although in the 1930s, times were too hard to serve more than dessert to the women who visited for an afternoon of cardplaying, today these weekly bridge games are regarded as an opportunity to display one's culinary skills.

In recalling what she had been served at a fellow bridge partner's home the previous week, one woman noted: "We always serve too much, I'm ashamed to tell you. Well, she brought out a composed plate for each one of us. On the plate was a stuffed tomato with chicken salad and a three-layered gelatin salad with strawberries in the bottom layer, cream cheese in the middle and pineapple and other fruits on top. Then, each plate also held an open-faced sandwich with tiny shrimp and a melted cheese sandwich. And of course, the bread was 'colored.' " (In Lynchburg this is bread that has been specially ordered from the bakery for parties and tinted pink, green, or some other pastel shade.)

She then described the dessert that followed: "Chocolate and vanilla ice cream with hot chocolate sauce, pecans and a cherry. Then, because the hostess was cutting down on calories, she only passed around homemade butter cookies as an accompaniment." My informant was quick to add that when the bridge club met at *her* house, there was always a tall angel food cake or fresh coconut layer cake for dessert.

Thus, it should come as no surprise that from the very beginning, dinner at Miss Mary's was a gastronomic treat. The noon-hour meal was dished up "family style." Guests sat down together, and platter upon platter of food was brought to the table. The dishes varied from day to day, depending both on Miss Mary's mood of the morning and on the season—what was fresh and available. But it was always Southern fare at its peak. Classic dishes, like fried chicken dipped in a rich egg batter, golden biscuits, or cheese grits, appeared often and were always accompanied by plenty of fresh vegetables. Desserts were almost always pies—fruit pies, custard pies, rolled-up pies—just about any kind of pie one could imagine. This was typical Southern cooking a hundred years ago . . . and it is still the food to be found in Lynchburg today.

It may come as a surprise to many to learn that distilled spirits cannot be sold in the town of Lynchburg. Therefore, no alcohol, not even Jack Daniel's, was served at the boardinghouse. (Miss Mary wouldn't have served it even had it been legal to do so since she didn't approve of drinking.) The only exception to this rule was at Christmas when Mary Bobo's special Boiled Custard, an eggnoglike beverage, was handed around to all guests. While the custard itself is nonalcoholic, a small crystal pitcher filled with Jack Daniel's was offered as the rich drink was served so that each guest could stir in an amount to taste.

Although Miss Mary is dead, the tradition is still carried on in her home, now a restaurant: Miss Mary Bobo's Boardinghouse.

There, her cooks prepare all the dishes following the same menus and recipes. Noontime dinner, by reservation only, is served five days a week. Some typical menus follow.

MENU

Pot Roast with Carrots
Salmon Croquettes
Baked Apples
Asparagus-Almond Casserole
Summer Squash Medley
Cheese-Topped Mashed Potatoes
Skillet Corn with Bacon
Creole Green Beans
Wilted Lettuce
Simmered Dried Beans
Corn Light Bread
Bobo House Buttermilk Pie

MENU

Southern Pork Ribs
Classic Southern Fried Chicken
Southern-Style Green Beans
Cabbage Slaw
Scalloped Potatoes
Fried Okra
Mustard and Turnip Greens
Stewed Tomato Casserole
Garlic Cheese Grits
Date Waldorf Salad
Skillet Corn Bread
"In the Hollow" Fresh Peach Cobbler with Ice Cream

INTRODUCTION

MENU

Stuffed Peppers
Chicken Spaghetti
Candied Sweet Potatoes
Hominy Casserole
Fried Green Tomatoes
Skillet Corn with Bacon
Southern-Style Green Beans
Spinach Prepared Like Poke Sallet
Cheese-Sauced Cauliflower
Fresh Tomato Aspic
Corn Muffins
Fudge Meringue Pie

MENU

BBQ Pork Chops
Creamed Chicken on Corn Bread
Franks and Kraut Casserole
Green Beans and Potatoes
Black-Eyed Peas
Baked Macaroni and Cheese
Cabbage Slaw
Special Squash Casserole
Buttermilk Biscuits
Baked Apples
Banana-Pecan Bread
Dump Cake with Ice Cream

You will find the recipes for all these dishes, and many more, throughout this book, which seeks to capture and preserve the essence of the fine food of Lynchburg, Tennessee.

February 28. Well this is not only Quarterly Meeting day, but it is fast morning as well. Mary, Eula and I fasted and Sion intended to but forgot it. We fasted at breakfast only. This morning Mary and I cooked until time for me to go to Church and we had a splendid dinner and not one person came home to dinner with me. Yet I never regret cooking good things and a quantity of them once in a while, so the children can have a share. They love good things and so do we who are older. If company stays away, we can always dispose of the rations. I sent Zella L. a nice waiter full of victuals.

Sue Dance Record's Diary, 1896.

MAIN DISHES
Meats, Poultry, & Fish

THE MAIN COURSE DISHES served at Miss Mary's will appeal to those who like simple, hearty fare—and plenty of it. People in these parts haven't heard of *nouvelle cuisine*—and even if they had, they'd probably turn up their noses in disdain.

Southern Fried Chicken was a favorite at Miss Mary's, so it was served often—always freshly cooked, crisp and golden. But chicken dishes didn't stop with this well-known classic. There were baked dishes, like Creamed Chicken and Broccoli Casserole, which layers tender chicken with fresh vegetables, as well as Chicken and Dumplings in a wholesome stew, and Creamed Chicken on Corn Bread. For special occasions, Barbecued Doves (Rock Cornish hens in less rural areas) were a real treat.

After chicken, pork was the most popular food. Guests welcomed Pork and Gravy—tender cutlets served over golden biscuits, and Miss Mary's BBQ Pork Chops went especially well with her Cabbage Slaw. Southern Pork Ribs were all-time favorites, and diners went through a lot of napkins in the course of that meal.

It's hard to buy fresh fish and other seafood in Lynchburg, as the town is inland and too tiny to support a fish store. However, Miss Mary created a special Luxurious Tuna Casserole, which contains fresh mushrooms, asparagus, and other vegetables to compensate for the fact that the fish is from a can. And she also served delectable, light Salmon Croquettes that almost melt in your mouth. Another favorite was freshwater fish (most often catfish), dipped in cornmeal and fried until tender and golden brown.

All of Mary Bobo's main course recipes will appeal as much to the home cook as to the guests who dined at her table, not only because they are appetizing, but also because most are remarkably quick and easy to make. The majority of the recipes call for few ingredients, and most are refreshingly economical as well—a real boon to the cook on a budget.

Country Fried Steak with Buttermilk Gravy

❖

Of all the many main course dishes I sampled from Mrs. Bobo's kitchen, this is perhaps my favorite—rich and satisfying, with a wonderfully thick gravy that almost makes itself. Country Fried Steak with Buttermilk Gravy is a true Southern classic—and once you try it, you'll understand why it is held in such esteem.

*2 pounds round steak
(purchase as thin a cut as
possible)
Salt and pepper
Flour
1 tablespoon vegetable oil
1 onion, chopped*

*1 cup water
1 cup buttermilk
1 cup shredded sharp Cheddar
cheese
Hot Buttermilk Biscuits (page
106) or "Riz" Biscuits (page
105)*

Cut the steak into serving-size pieces. If cut is not very thin, pound lightly. Season with salt and pepper and dredge in flour, shaking off the excess.

Heat the oil in a large skillet and brown the meat on both sides. Add the onion and continue cooking until the onion is translucent but not brown. Add the water and cook a couple of minutes, scraping up any browned bits from the skillet. Add the buttermilk and stir in well. Cook, covered, over low heat until the meat is tender, about 1 hour.

Just before serving, stir in the Cheddar cheese. Serve meat and gravy over hot biscuits.

Yield: 6 to 8 servings.

Pot Roast with Carrots

❖

This simple, homey oven-braised beef pot roast is immensely satisfying on a cold night. It's an economical one-pot meal for most families, although at Miss Mary's it was served with lots of accompaniments, like her Baked Macaroni and Cheese (page 82), Baked Apples (page 86), and Skillet Corn with Bacon (page 74).

2-pound beef chuck roast
1 tablespoon vegetable oil
Salt and pepper
1 clove garlic, minced
2 onions, sliced
1 pound carrots, peeled and
  cut into 2-inch lengths
4 potatoes, peeled and
  quartered

2½ cups boiling water
2 tablespoons cornstarch,
  dissolved in 2 tablespoons
  water
1 teaspoon Worcestershire
  sauce

In a heavy ovenproof skillet or Dutch oven, brown the meat on all sides in a little oil. Season with salt and pepper. Add the garlic and onions to the pan. If you like your vegetables very tender, add the carrots and potatoes at this point; if you prefer firmer vegetables, add after 1 hour of baking. Add the boiling water, cover, and place in a 350° oven. Bake until the meat and vegetables are tender, about 2 hours altogether.

Remove the meat and vegetables from the pot. Cut the meat into serving-size portions. Remove any fat from the top of the cooking liquid and bring liquid to a boil on the top of the stove. Add the cornstarch mixture and cook, stirring, for a few minutes until the liquid thickens. Season with Worcestershire sauce and

additional salt and pepper, if desired. Return the meat and vegetables to the pot and heat through before serving.

Yield: 6 servings.

Wild Onion. Indians believed the wild onion to be
a fast-acting cure for colds, taken as a strong tea. It
makes a delicious onion soup; it is also fine in salads,
with its curative properties not abused by cooking.

On Man and the Good Life. Leaves from the Notebook
of Emmett Gowen. Being a rather loose collection of
writings, notes and folk beliefs on the delights of farming and other subjects related to our earth and Tennessee
in particular. Published by the Lynchburg Hardware and
General Store, 1974.

Pepper Meat Loaf

❖

This lusciously moist meat loaf is also delightfully crunchy because of the crispy bits of bell pepper scattered throughout. When the loaf is partially baked, a slightly tart tomato sauce is poured over it, and it continues to cook while absorbing the delicious flavors of the savory sauce. Miss Mary's meat loaf is even better when accompanied by one of her heartier starch dishes, such as Garlic Cheese Grits (page 85) or Cheese-Topped Mashed Potatoes (page 77).

Meat Loaf

2 eggs
½ 10¾-ounce can condensed
   cream of mushroom soup
¼ teaspoon salt
⅛ teaspoon pepper

1 pound ground beef
1 small onion, minced
2 bell peppers, finely diced
2 tablespoons catsup

Tomato Sauce

1 onion, diced
2 stalks celery, diced
2 tablespoons butter or
   margarine

1 16-ounce can whole
   tomatoes, undrained and
   chopped
2 tablespoons cider vinegar

To make the meat loaf, beat the eggs lightly in a large bowl. Add the mushroom soup, salt, and pepper and mix well. Add the remaining ingredients and toss with a fork until well mixed.

Turn the meat mixture into a 9 by 5-inch loaf pan and pat to make even. Bake the loaf in a 350° oven 45 minutes. Pour off any fat that accumulates around the sides.

Meanwhile, to make the sauce, sauté the onion and celery in butter or margarine until tender. Stir in the tomatoes and vinegar and simmer, uncovered, 10 minutes.

Pour the tomato sauce over the meat loaf, letting it run down the sides. Bake 30 minutes longer.

Yield: 4 servings.

January 3. Visited the sick. This is a great day with our little family, being the birthday of Mr. R. He would say that he was 37 years old today but in reality he is 47 (he wants to be just even with me). Well something must be done, and we knew he would appreciate an o'possum dinner as much as anything we could cook. Sion and Dance had bought one in town there weeks before and it had fattened nicely, so we gave him a "big fat possum" for dinner. He ate it and his hare and appreciated it very much.

Sue Dance Record's Diary, 1896.

Stuffed Peppers

❖

A classic version of everyone's favorite ground beef dish, these good, hearty peppers are rich with the flavor of Cheddar cheese.

6 nice-sized bell peppers
Salt
1 pound ground beef
1 onion, chopped
Pepper
1 16-ounce can whole tomatoes, undrained and chopped

½ cup water
¾ cup uncooked rice
1 teaspoon Worcestershire sauce
1 cup shredded sharp Cheddar cheese

Cut a thin slice off the top of the peppers and remove the core and seeds. Dice the tops and reserve. Drop the peppers into a large pot of boiling water and cook until tender, about 5 minutes. Remove from the water and place in a greased shallow baking dish. Season the insides with salt.

In a large skillet, brown the ground beef with the onion and reserved green pepper. (There will probably be enough fat in the beef so that it's not necessary to add oil to the skillet; if not, add 1 tablespoon oil.) Cook until the meat is browned and the onion tender. Drain off any excess fat. Season with salt and pepper; add tomatoes, water, rice, and Worcestershire sauce.

Bring the skillet contents to a boil. Cover and lower the heat. Cook until the rice is tender, about 20 minutes. Remove from the heat and stir in the cheese.

Stuff the beef mixture into the peppers. Bake the peppers in a 350° oven 30 minutes.

Yield: 6 servings.

38

Pork and Gravy

❖

Here's a real down-home dish that's very easy to cook. Tender pork cutlets are sautéed and then simmered in liquid that will eventually form a hearty gravy. At Miss Mary's the dish was served with hot biscuits, such as her Buttermilk Biscuits (page 106) or "Riz" Biscuits (page 105).

2 pounds pork cutlets (from the shoulder—also called tenderloin)
Salt
Pepper
Flour for dredging, plus 3 tablespoons for gravy
2 tablespoons vegetable oil
1 cup water
¾ cup milk

Cut the pork into serving-size pieces (there should be about 8). Season lightly with salt and pepper and dip into flour. Shake off the excess. Brown the pork in batches in oil in a heavy skillet, removing the meat as it cooks.

After all the pork has cooked, return all meat to the skillet and add the water. Cook, covered, over low heat 30 minutes.

Remove the meat from the pan. Dissolve 3 tablespoons flour in the milk. Bring the liquid in the skillet to a boil and add the milk and flour mixture. Cook, stirring, until the gravy thickens. Return the meat to the pan, season with additional salt and pepper, if necessary, and heat through.

Yield: 6 to 8 servings.

BBQ Pork Chops

❖

These pork chops were very popular at Miss Mary's. They're easy to fix and juicy and tender, with a hearty flavor that comes from the barbecue basting sauce.

1 onion, chopped
½ tablespoon butter
¼ cup water
½ cup catsup
2 tablespoons distilled white vinegar

1 tablespoon light or dark molasses
⅛ teaspoon hot pepper sauce
6 pork chops
Salt and pepper

In a small saucepan, sauté the onion in butter until softened. Add the water, catsup, vinegar, molasses, and pepper sauce. Simmer the barbecue sauce, stirring occasionally, 20 minutes.

Meanwhile, brown the pork chops lightly on both sides in a skillet (there should be enough fat on the meat so that no oil will be required; if the chops are particularly lean, add up to 1 tablespoon vegetable oil to the skillet). Transfer to a shallow baking pan and sprinkle lightly with salt and pepper. Bake the chops, covered, in a 350° oven 45 minutes.

Drain off any fat from the baking pan and spread the barbecue sauce over the chops. Cover and return to the oven for 15 minutes longer.

Yield: 6 servings.

Southern Pork Ribs

❖

Southern pork ribs are hearty and meaty. Minimal seasoning—just salt, black pepper, and red pepper—is all that's needed to bring out their simple rich flavor. This is a meal for people with good appetites; just be sure to fix plenty of ribs.

3 pounds meaty pork ribs (often called "country-style" ribs)

½ teaspoon red pepper flakes Salt and pepper

Place the ribs in a large saucepan and add enough water to cover them. Add the red pepper flakes and about 1 teaspoon salt. Bring to a boil. Then lower the heat, cover, and simmer until the ribs are tender, about 45 minutes.

Remove the ribs from the pot and place them meaty side up in a large baking pan. Season with salt and pepper. Bake in a 400° oven until browned, about 20 minutes.

Yield: 4 servings.

Ham Casserole

❖

Here's a quick and easy way to make use of leftover holiday ham. The casserole is colorful, economical, and nutritious. The Cheddar cheese sauce lends a wonderfully hearty flavor to the ham, while the broccoli adds an attractive green contrast.

2 tablespoons butter	1 bunch broccoli (2 or 3
2 tablespoons flour	stalks)
1 cup milk	8 ounces spaghetti, cooked
2 cups shredded Cheddar	until tender and drained
cheese	2 cups diced cooked ham
¼ teaspoon pepper	

Melt the butter in a medium saucepan. Stir in the flour. Add the milk and cook, stirring, until the sauce thickens and comes to a boil. Add the cheese and pepper and cook, stirring, until the cheese has melted. Remove from the heat.

Trim the tough ends off the broccoli. Cut the broccoli lengthwise into quarters. Cook in boiling water or steam until tender, about 20 minutes. Drain and chop coarsely.

When the spaghetti has cooked, stir in the cheese sauce. Add the ham and broccoli. Turn the mixture into a greased 2-quart casserole. Bake, covered, in a 350° oven 40 minutes, or until hot and bubbly.

Yield: 4 servings.

Franks and Kraut Casserole

❖

Here's an easy-to-fix main course dish that's a favorite with adults and kids alike. Sauerkraut and franks are layered in a casserole and covered with spicy tomato sauce before baking.

1 onion, chopped
1 tablespoon vegetable oil
¾ cup water
¾ cup catsup
2 tablespoons light or dark
   brown sugar
½ teaspoon dry mustard
1 16-ounce can sauerkraut,
   drained
1 pound frankfurters

In a small saucepan, cook the onion in the oil until tender. Add the water, catsup, brown sugar, and mustard and cook, stirring, until the mixture comes to a boil. Remove from the heat.

In a greased 1½-quart casserole, spread the sauerkraut in an even layer. Place the frankfurters on top and pour the sauce over all.

Bake the casserole, covered, in a 375° oven 30 minutes.

Yield: 4 servings.

January 13. Monday morning. It seems that on Monday, new resolutions for work are entered into by every family and plans set up that will accomplish the greatest ends—and so on this day. After breakfast and house cleaning, an old goods box containing a variety of scraps of every conceivable shape and color was brought in to the family to be cut in quilt pieces. Here was a piece of a dress of a friend, there another valuable piece simply because a loved one wore something like it, but prized above all is the big roll of scraps that Grandma R. brought the children. She often said she wanted to treat all just alike, showing no partiality, and now that she is dead and in "Heaven" each one must have their share of the pieces. So they are put aside to be divided. Pieces for seven quilts are being cut and the old box is growing empty.

Sue Dance Record's Diary, 1896.

Classic Southern Fried Chicken

❖

Mary Bobo said, "This is the best fried chicken you'll ever eat!" and she sure was right about that. Delicately crisp and browned on the outside, moist and tender within, this chicken makes you wonder if it would ever be possible to eat "take-out" again.

*1 2½ to 3-pound frying
   chicken, cut into pieces
2 eggs
½ cup milk*

*About 1½ cups flour, seasoned
   with ¼ teaspoon salt and
⅛ teaspoon pepper
2 cups corn oil*

Place the chicken pieces in a large bowl of salted water and let sit 10 minutes. Drain and pat dry.

Beat together the eggs and the milk and place in a shallow bowl. Dip the chicken pieces in the egg mixture and then roll in the seasoned flour. Shake off any excess flour.

Heat the oil in a large heavy pot to about 350°. If you don't have a deep-fat frying thermometer, drop a 1-inch cube of bread into the fat. If it's crisp and browned in 1 minute, the oil is at the right temperature. If the temperature of the oil is too low, the chicken will be soggy; if too high, it will burn.

Cook the chicken pieces, a few at a time (do not crowd), in the hot oil until crisp and browned, about 15 to 17 minutes. Drain on paper towels. Keep cooked chicken warm in a 200° oven while remaining pieces cook.

   Yield: 4 servings.

Creamed Chicken on Corn Bread

❖

In the South, "corn bread" refers to any cornmeal batter, whether baked in a skillet, muffin tins, or corn stick pans. In this recipe, the corn bread takes the form of lovely browned muffins topped by cooked chicken in a rich cream sauce, a dish that is especially pleasing on a cold winter night.

Chicken

1 chicken, about 3½ pounds
6 cups water
1 teaspoon salt
6 peppercorns
1 stalk celery, sliced
⅓ cup (5⅓ tablespoons) butter
⅓ cup flour
1½ cups light cream or half and half

1 tablespoon grated onion
1 10-ounce package frozen green peas, thawed
1 4-ounce jar pimientos, diced
½ teaspoon sage
¼ teaspoon pepper
1 teaspoon Worcestershire sauce

Corn Muffins

¾ cup flour
2½ teaspoons baking powder
1 tablespoon sugar
½ teaspoon salt
1¼ cups cornmeal, preferably white

1 egg, beaten
2 tablespoons butter, melted
1 cup milk

Place the chicken in a large pot with the water, salt, peppercorns, and celery. Bring to a boil. Then lower the heat, cover and simmer 45 minutes, or until the chicken is tender. When the

46

chicken is cool enough to handle, remove the skin and bones and dice the meat. Reserve 1½ cups broth.

In a large heavy saucepan, melt the butter. Add the flour and stir until bubbly. Add the cream and reserved broth. Cook, stirring, until the mixture thickens and comes to a boil. Stir in the cooked chicken, grated onion, peas, pimientos, sage, pepper, and Worcestershire sauce. Keep warm over low heat while preparing the muffins.

In a bowl, stir together the flour, baking powder, sugar, salt, and cornmeal. In another bowl, stir together the egg, melted butter, and milk. Add to the dry ingredients and stir just until moistened.

Divide the batter among 12 greased muffin tins. Bake the muffins in a 425° oven about 25 minutes, or until a toothpick inserted in the center comes out clean.

To serve, place 2 muffins on a plate and split open. Butter, if desired. Spoon the creamed chicken over.

Yield: 6 servings.

Chicken and Dumplings

❖

Most dumplings are puffy little balls, but those from Miss Mary's kitchen were hearty squares of flavorful homemade pasta dough. They're cooked and served in a rich chicken broth that also contains chunks of the chicken used to make it.

1 chicken, about 3½ to 4 pounds	¼ teaspoon pepper
6 cups water	2 cups flour
2½ teaspoons salt, divided	1 egg
	3 tablespoons butter, melted

In a large saucepan, combine the chicken with the water, 2 teaspoons salt, and the pepper. Bring to a boil. Then lower the heat and simmer, covered, until the chicken is tender, about 45 minutes.

Skim the fat from the broth. Remove the chicken, discard the skin and bones, and cut the meat into bite-size pieces. Return the chicken to the broth. Remove ⅓ cup broth and let cool to room temperature.

In a bowl, stir together the flour and the remaining ½ teaspoon salt. With a fork, beat in the egg, then the melted butter. Stir in the reserved broth and knead the dough for a few minutes, until it is smooth.

Working with half the dough at a time, roll out on a lightly floured surface to the thickness of pie pastry. Cut into 1-inch by 2-inch rectangles and let dry in a single layer 15 minutes.

Bring the broth to a slow boil. Add the dumplings and cook, stirring, until tender, about 5 minutes. Serve in deep soup bowls.

Yield: 4 to 6 servings.

Chicken Salad Casserole

❖

This hearty, homey casserole tastes like hot chicken salad, complete with crunchy celery, onion bits, and mayonnaise.

1 chicken, about 3½ pounds, quartered	¼ cup mayonnaise
About 6 cups water	1 cup diced celery
1 teaspoon salt	¼ cup minced onion
6 peppercorns	¼ teaspoon pepper
1 10¾-ounce can condensed cream of mushroom soup	¾ cup bread crumbs or corn-bread crumbs

Place the chicken in a large saucepan with enough water to just cover it. Add the salt and peppercorns. Bring to a boil. Lower the heat, cover, and simmer until the chicken is tender, about 45 minutes. Remove the chicken from the liquid (reserve the broth for another purpose). When the chicken is cool enough to handle, remove the skin and bones and dice the meat.

Mix the chicken with all other ingredients except the crumbs and turn into a greased 1½-quart round casserole.

Bake the casserole in a 325° oven 40 minutes. Sprinkle with the crumbs and bake 10 minutes longer.

Yield: 4 servings.

Chicken Spaghetti

❖

This traditional Southern recipe differs from the chicken-noodle recipes served in other parts of the country because of the large quantity of broth that goes into the dish before it's baked. The broth adds a wonderful flavor to the casserole and also gives it a slightly soupy quality. This dish is easy to fix and has the sort of homey flavor that everyone will find appealing.

For the Chicken

1 chicken, about 3½ pounds, quartered	*1 teaspoon salt*
	6 peppercorns
6 cups water	*2 bay leaves*

For the Casserole

8 ounces thin spaghetti, cooked until barely tender and drained	*1 4-ounce jar pimientos, drained and diced*
	1 cup diced celery
1 10¾-ounce can condensed cream of mushroom soup	*½ teaspoon salt*
	¼ teaspoon pepper

In a large pot, combine all the ingredients for the chicken. Bring to a boil. Reduce the heat, cover, and simmer 45 minutes, or until the chicken is tender.

Skin and bone the chicken and cut it into large dice. There should be about 4 cups. Skim the fat from the broth, remove and discard the bay leaves and peppercorns, and measure 4 cups of broth (reserve remaining broth for another use).

Combine all ingredients for the casserole with the cooked

chicken and broth and turn into a greased 2½-quart round casserole.

Bake the casserole in a 350° oven about 1¼ hours, or until the broth has mostly been absorbed.

Yield: 6 servings.

January 19. This day nineteen years ago I went with my new husband to his Mother's. We had a fearful road to travel on account of the big snow which had fallen two weeks before on the night of Dec. 31st and while it had melted on all the roads, there was still plenty of snow on the hills. However we reached our destination, forty-two miles distant, by five o'clock. Then I met for the first time in my life any of the family except my husband. I felt a little peculiar, but not embarrassed, for Sister Abner and all the relatives present on that occasion treated me with such marked kindness that I felt that I was more than welcome in my new sphere, and time has proven that I was not mistaken. Ma gave us a splendid reception; she did not undertake to have a large crowd but had a nice supper and plenty of it. They found me out that night for I was hungry and ate until I was satisfied. All in all we had a most delightful trip.

Sue Dance Record's Diary, 1896.

Barbecued Rock Cornish Hens

❖

This recipe originally called for doves, but since these may be difficult to find, I've substituted the more readily available Rock Cornish hens. The hens aren't actually barbecued, but rather poached until tender and then finished off in a sauce that contains many of the ingredients of a barbecue marinade. The hens are traditionally served with Garlic Cheese Grits (page 85).

4 Rock Cornish hens, thawed
  if frozen
2 quarts water
2 teaspoons salt
3 tablespoons butter
3 tablespoons flour
1 tablespoon sugar
¼ teaspoon pepper

2 tablespoons distilled white
  vinegar
1½ tablespoons Worcester-
  shire sauce
1 tablespoon freshly squeezed
  lemon juice
¼ teaspoon hot pepper sauce

Place the hens in a large pot with the water and salt. Bring to a boil. Then reduce the heat, cover, and simmer 45 minutes, or until tender. Remove the hens from the broth and keep them warm. Skim the fat from the broth and reserve 2½ cups for the sauce (save the remainder for another use, if desired).

Melt the butter in a large skillet. Stir in the flour and cook, stirring, 2 minutes. Add the reserved broth, along with all remaining ingredients. Cook, stirring, until the sauce comes to a boil and thickens slightly.

Add the hens to the skillet and cook, basting, until thoroughly heated through.

Yield: 4 servings.

Creamed Chicken and Broccoli Casserole

❖

Here's another chicken casserole, this one made quite elegant with the addition of freshly cooked broccoli stalks. It's a good dish for a party because it can be made ahead of time and reheated just before serving.

1 chicken, about 3½ pounds, quartered
1 teaspoon salt
6 peppercorns
Water
2 stalks celery, diced
1 onion, chopped
5 tablespoons butter, divided
¼ cup flour
1½ cups light cream
¼ teaspoon sage
⅛ teaspoon pepper
1 teaspoon lemon juice
1 bunch broccoli
½ cup shredded Cheddar cheese
⅓ cup bread crumbs

Place the chicken, salt, and peppercorns in a large pot. Add enough water to nearly cover the chicken. Bring to a boil. Lower the heat, cover, and cook until the chicken is tender, about 45 minutes. Remove the chicken from the broth and when it is cool enough to handle, discard the skin and bones and dice the meat. Skim the fat from the broth and reserve 1½ cups (the remaining broth may be saved for another purpose).

In another saucepan, sauté the celery and onion in 4 tablespoons butter until tender. Stir in the flour until well blended. Add the reserved broth and light cream. Cook, stirring constantly, until the sauce comes to a boil and thickens slightly. Season with the sage, pepper, and lemon juice. Stir in the chicken.

Cut the tough bottom portion from the broccoli and cut the stalks lengthwise, so as to make long, thin stalks. Place in a pot of boiling water and cook until almost tender, about 15 minutes. Drain well.

Place the broccoli stalks in a greased 3-quart casserole. Cover with the chicken and sauce mixture. Sprinkle with the Cheddar cheese and then with the bread crumbs. Dot with the remaining 1 tablespoon butter.

Bake the casserole in a 350° oven 45 minutes, or until hot and bubbly.

Yield: 6 servings.

Luxurious Tuna Casserole

❖

Here the traditional tuna-noodle casserole is made extra-special with the addition of fresh mushrooms and asparagus and lots of Cheddar cheese. It's really fancy enough for guests, but then that's just who dined at Mary Bobo's table every day.

12 ounces mushrooms, sliced	1 12-ounce can tuna, drained
½ stick (¼ cup) butter	and flaked
¼ cup flour	1 10-ounce package frozen
2¼ cups milk	peas, defrosted
¼ teaspoon salt	1 pound asparagus
⅛ teaspoon pepper	8 ounces egg noodles
2 cups shredded Cheddar	½ cup bread crumbs
cheese	

In a medium saucepan, cook the mushrooms in the butter. At first the mushrooms will give off a lot of liquid. Continue cooking until most of that liquid evaporates and the moisture left in the pan is melted butter. Add the flour and mix it in well. Add the milk and cook, stirring, until the mixture comes to a boil and thickens. Add the salt, pepper, and Cheddar cheese. Cook, stirring, until the cheese melts. Remove from the heat and stir in the tuna and peas.

Trim the asparagus and cook in boiling water until tender, about 8 minutes. Drain well.

Cook the noodles in a large pot of boiling water until tender. Drain well. Add the noodles to the tuna mixture and mix well.

Grease a 3-quart casserole and spread one third of the tuna mixture in it. Arrange one third of the asparagus on top. Repeat the layers twice more. Sprinkle the top with bread crumbs.

Bake the casserole in a 350° oven 45 minutes, or until hot and bubbly.

Yield: 6 servings.

Fried Fish

❖

Lynchburg, being an inland town, does not have ready access to saltwater fish, but the people there do eat a great deal of fresh-water fish, such as catfish, crappie, bream, or bass. Generally the fish are prepared quite simply—seasoned with salt and pepper, dipped into cornmeal, and fried until crisp and tender. It may seem plain, but the flavor sure is good!

*Small whole fish or fish fillets
    from larger fish
Salt and pepper*

*White cornmeal
Bacon drippings or vegetable
    oil*

Season the fish with salt and pepper and dip into cornmeal to coat well.

Heat ½-inch-deep bacon drippings or oil in a skillet until quite hot. Add the fish, being careful not to crowd them. Cook over medium heat until browned on the bottom. Turn and cook the other side until browned. The fish will take about 5 minutes on each side.

Salmon Croquettes

❖

These tender, light fried morsels make a wonderful supper or lunch dish, because they are satisfying and flavorful without being overly filling.

3 tablespoons butter
1/3 cup flour
1 cup milk
1/8 teaspoon salt
1/8 teaspoon pepper
1 16-ounce can salmon

1 egg, beaten
2 tablespoons freshly squeezed
   lemon juice
About 2 cups fine cracker
   crumbs
Oil for deep frying

Melt the butter in a saucepan. Stir in the flour. Add the milk and cook, stirring, until the mixture thickens and comes to a boil. Season with salt and pepper. Drain and flake the salmon, discarding the skin and bones. Add the salmon to the sauce, along with the egg and lemon juice. Refrigerate the mixture for at least 1 hour.

Form the chilled mixture into balls about 1½ inches in diameter and roll in the cracker crumbs. Chill for at least another hour. Just before frying, roll balls in crumbs again.

Heat the oil in a large heavy skillet or saucepan until hot. Add the croquettes, a few at a time, and cook until browned, about 6 minutes. Drain on paper towels and place in a warm oven while others cook.

Yield: about 20 croquettes, or 4 servings.

Vegetables, Salads,
& Side Dishes

ONE OF THE MOST enjoyable aspects of dinner at Mary Bobo's was the fact that the meal was always served "family style," so that everyone had the opportunity to sample a bit of every dish and even take "seconds." And each day, to the delight of everyone present, eight to ten different vegetable, salad, and side dishes were placed on the table. It took a good quarter-hour just to pass all the dishes around so the diners could fill their plates.

Vegetable dishes included such traditional fare as Green Beans with Bacon, Fried Corn or tender slices of okra dipped in cornmeal and deep-fried. Baked vegetables, like Summer Squash Medley, rich with Cheddar cheese, were also offered. And that old Southern specialty, long-simmered Mustard and Turnip Greens, might appear on the table, too. There was a garden behind Miss Mary's house, so the vegetables served at the noon meal were likely still growing under the sun that very morning.

Lots of salads were also to be found on Miss Mary's table, but not the usual tossed salad. When greens were served—and they were served only in the early spring, when the leaves are at their tenderest—the bacon-flavored dressing was generally *hot*, which only made the greens more appealing.

With the exception of a few classics like Cabbage Slaw and Potato Salad, most of the salads in Miss Mary's collection are made from gelatin and hence are on the sweet side. They're colorfully attractive and may contain a variety of fruits and nuts, as well as rich dairy products, like whipped cream or cream cheese. These salads go well with plain meats and lend a festive flair to the table.

Finally, there are hearty side dishes, like creamy Macaroni and Cheese or Hominy Casserole. And if you've never sampled grits, Mary Bobo's Garlic Cheese Grits turn what's normally simple breakfast fare into a flavorful creation. Another side dish, so popular that it appeared on the table almost daily, was Miss Mary's Baked Apples, which are meant to be eaten as a sweet relish.

All these vegetables are so filling and satisfying that they really let you know you've eaten. After a couple of helpings of Cheese-Topped Mashed Potatoes, you wonder if you'll have room for dessert—until, of course, it's actually there to tempt you.

While few home cooks would relish the notion of making a half-dozen different vegetable dishes to accompany a single meal, one or two of Miss Mary's specialties will definitely enliven anything else you happen to be serving.

Summer Squash Medley

❖

Vegetables seldom came to Miss Mary's table unadorned. Here's a good example of one of her highly praised vegetable dishes. Tender yellow summer squash is tossed with sautéed onions and peppers and then enveloped in a rich cheese custard. The medley is turned into a casserole and baked until golden. This casserole goes well with any simple entrée and would certainly add zest to a plain meal.

1 pound yellow summer squash (about 2 medium or 6 tiny), cut into ½-inch slices
1 onion, finely diced
1 green pepper, finely diced
2 tablespoons butter

1 egg, beaten
1 cup plus 2 tablespoons shredded sharp Cheddar cheese, divided
¼ teaspoon salt
⅛ teaspoon pepper

Place the squash in a saucepan. Add just enough water to cover. Bring the water to a boil, cover the pan, reduce to a simmer and cook just until the squash is tender, about 5 minutes. Drain well.

In a small skillet, sauté the onion and pepper in the butter until tender and lightly browned. Add to the squash, along with the egg, 1 cup Cheddar cheese, salt, and pepper. Toss gently.

Turn the squash into a greased 1½-quart round casserole and sprinkle with the remaining 2 tablespoons cheese. Bake the casserole in a 350° oven until lightly browned, about 30 minutes.

Yield: 4 servings.

Special Squash Casserole

❖

In Lynchburg, when someone wants to describe a favorite dish, they'll say, "It's *real* special." And that's just what this creamy, rich squash casserole is. Ordinary yellow squash is transformed into fare worthy of your most special guests. Miss Mary picked the squash from her garden when they were quite tiny—not much bigger than a thumb, in fact. If you can't find such young squash, buy the youngest and tenderest available. Because the casserole is somewhat liquid (rather like the texture of creamed spinach), you'll probably wish to serve it in small bowls.

1 pound yellow summer squash (about 6 tiny or 2 to 3 medium), cut into ½-inch slices
2 carrots, peeled and sliced
1 onion, chopped
2 cups ¼-inch firm white bread cubes (about 3 slices)
3 tablespoons butter

3 tablespoons flour
1½ cups chicken broth
1 8-ounce carton sour cream
¼ teaspoon sage
1 jar (about 7 ounces) pimientos, drained and chopped
½ cup fresh bread crumbs

Place the squash, carrots, and onion in a saucepan. Add water to cover. Bring to a boil. Lower the heat, cover, and simmer until the vegetables are tender, about 20 minutes. Drain and mash.

Meanwhile, spread the bread cubes on a baking sheet and bake in a 350° oven about 10 minutes, until crisp.

Melt the butter in a medium saucepan. Stir in the flour. Add the chicken broth. Cook, stirring constantly, until the mixture comes to a boil and thickens. Remove from the heat. Stir in the sour cream, sage, and pimientos. Then stir in the mashed vegetables.

Sprinkle the bread cubes on the bottom of a greased 1½-quart casserole and spread the squash mixture over them. Sprinkle with the bread crumbs.

Bake the casserole in a 350° oven 30 minutes, or until it is bubbly hot.

Yield: 8 servings.

April 16. I have been busy today making soap and attending to the necessary duties in connection therewith. I also planted butter beans, squashes and cucumbers. Sion ploughed a good deal, planted corn and beans, etc. and attended school besides. Dance helped—I do love to see boys work with a willing heart and ready hand. They went fishing tonight and caught some nice catfish.

Sue Dance Record's Diary, 1896.

Cheese-Sauced Cauliflower

❖

Here's another fresh vegetable dish that's just one more reason people always remember the side dishes served at Miss Mary's table. The sauce is so good and simple to make that you'll find yourself using it for lots of other vegetables—try it over broccoli for starters.

1 head cauliflower, broken into flowerets	⅛ teaspoon salt
3 tablespoons butter or margarine	Dash pepper
3 tablespoons flour	½ cup shredded Cheddar cheese
1 cup milk	¼ teaspoon paprika

Cook the cauliflower in a large saucepan of boiling salted water until tender, about 5 minutes. Drain.

Meanwhile, in a small saucepan, melt the butter. Stir in the flour and then add the milk. Cook, stirring, until the sauce thickens and comes to a boil. Remove from the heat and season with the salt and pepper.

Turn the cauliflower into a large, shallow serving bowl. Cover with the white sauce and sprinkle with the cheese and then the paprika. Serve immediately.

Yield: 4 servings.

Asparagus–Almond Casserole

❖

Here's a luxurious treatment for a vegetable that's special no matter how it's served. Tender asparagus stalks are combined in a casserole with a creamy white sauce, crunchy toasted almonds, and lots of rich Cheddar cheese. The dish can be assembled in advance and baked just before serving.

½ cup slivered almonds
1 pound asparagus, trimmed
  of tough bottoms
4 tablespoons butter, divided
3 tablespoons flour

2 cups milk
¼ teaspoon salt
1½ cups shredded sharp
  Cheddar cheese
2 tablespoons cracker crumbs

In an ungreased skillet or an oven heated to 375°, toast the almonds until lightly browned. Set aside.

Cook the asparagus in boiling water until just tender, about 8 minutes. Drain.

Heat 3 tablespoons butter in a saucepan. Stir in the flour until well blended. Add the milk and cook, stirring constantly, until the sauce thickens and comes to a boil. Season with salt and remove from heat.

Place half the asparagus stalks in a greased, shallow casserole or baking pan. Sprinkle with half the cheese and then half the almonds. Pour half the sauce over. Repeat the layers. Sprinkle with the cracker crumbs and dot with the remaining 1 tablespoon butter.

Bake the casserole in a 375° oven until hot and bubbly, about 20 minutes.

Yield: 4 to 6 servings.

Fried Okra

❖

Okra, one of the most popular of all Southern vegetables, is found in plentiful supply in almost every supermarket south of the Mason-Dixon Line. In other parts of the country, though, it is a relative rarity, except in the grocer's freezer case.

Of all okra dishes, Fried Okra was the favorite at Miss Mary's table, as elsewhere throughout the South. There's good reason for this, for Fried Okra is crisp and golden on the outside, with a wonderful cornmeal flavor, and delectably tender within.

*1 10-ounce box frozen sliced
    okra, thawed, or 1½ cups
    sliced fresh okra*
Salt and pepper, to taste

*About ½ cup cornmeal,
    preferably white*
*Lard or vegetable oil for
    frying*

Let frozen okra drain in a colander for 30 minutes (fresh okra need not be drained). Season with salt and pepper.

Place okra in a bowl and add enough cornmeal to coat each slice.

Heat ½ inch of lard or oil in a heavy skillet, preferably cast iron. When oil is hot, add okra one layer deep. Cook until browned on one side, about 5 minutes, and then turn and cook on the other side. Drain on paper towels.

When all the okra has been cooked, heat briefly in a hot oven and serve immediately.

Yield: 4 to 6 servings.

Southern-Style Green Beans

❖

According to Southern tradition some vegetables, such as green beans, are usually cooked until meltingly tender. Although a far cry from the "al dente" beans currently enjoying so much popularity among many Americans, Southern-Style Green Beans have a character all their own. The original recipe specifies cooking the beans for a full three hours, which is possibly a bit excessive, but if you want to sample the true regional fare, you'll give the beans at least an hour to simmer with the bacon.

People in Lynchburg are very fond of dried red peppers in their cooking and most families who have gardens grow their own pepper plants. The fresh young peppers are strung up on string and left to dry. For those who don't have ready access to dried red peppers, ¼ teaspoon (or more, to taste) hot pepper sauce or dried red pepper flakes may be substituted.

For a true taste of Southern cooking, serve this dish with Garlic Cheese Grits (page 85).

1 pound fresh green beans
2 slices bacon, cut into small pieces (salt-cured country bacon is preferable to smoked bacon)
½ teaspoon salt

1 dried red pepper (or substitute ¼-½ teaspoon hot pepper sauce)
Pinch sugar
⅔ cup water

Trim the beans and break into about 1-inch lengths. Place in a saucepan with all other ingredients.

Bring the water to a boil. Reduce heat, cover, and simmer at least 1 hour, or until beans are of desired degree of tenderness. Remove red pepper before serving.

Yield: 4 servings.

Creole Green Beans

❖

Green pepper, onion, and tomatoes give this colorful vegetable dish a distinctive Creole flavor. It goes well with all types of meat, and any leftovers can be reheated successfully.

½ pound green beans,
trimmed
2 stalks celery, diced
1 green pepper, diced
1 onion, diced
2 tablespoons vegetable oil

1 28-ounce can tomatoes,
drained and coarsely
chopped
½ teaspoon sugar
⅛ teaspoon salt
⅛ teaspoon pepper

Cut the beans in half crosswise and then lengthwise (as for French-cut beans). Place in a large saucepan. Add water to cover. Bring to a boil and cook, covered, until the beans are tender. Drain and return beans to the pot.

In a large skillet, sauté the celery, green peppers, and onion in oil until tender and lightly brown. Add the tomatoes and simmer, uncovered, 15 minutes, or until most of the liquid has evaporated.

Add the sautéed vegetables to the pot with the beans, along with the sugar, salt, and pepper. Heat through.

Yield: 6 to 8 servings.

Green Beans and Potatoes

❖

Only four ingredients go into this simple, homey dish, yet the result is a complex of flavors that marry beautifully. It's a good accompaniment to roast meats and is especially convenient, as it combines the vegetable and starch courses into one.

1 pound green beans, trimmed
*   and halved*
6 slices bacon

1 teaspoon salt
6 to 8 new potatoes, peeled
*   and halved*

Place the green beans, bacon, and salt in a large pot and add water to just cover the beans. Bring to a boil. Lower the heat and cook, uncovered, at a slow boil 20 minutes.

Add the potatoes and enough additional water to cover all vegetables. Continue cooking until the potatoes and beans are very tender, at least 20 minutes longer.

Drain any water that remains and serve immediately.

Yield: 6 to 8 servings.

Pokeweed. When pokeweed shoots come up like asparagus in the spring, and are eaten as boiled greens, they are delicious and rate as a health food, especially good for rheumatism in older people with poor dietary habits. The young, tender shoots and leaves should be parboiled a few minutes and that water thrown away.

Pokeweed root and sulphur is a folk cure for itch. But, oh, it will burn. Of this remedy, my peasant informant said that his parents had to run the children down in a ten-acre field to catch them to apply the remedy; but it cured instantly and without fail.

On Man and the Good Life. Leaves from the Notebook of Emmett Gowen.

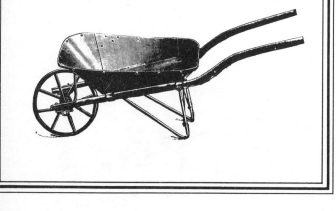

Spinach Prepared Like Poke Sallet

❖

Poke sallet is a weed that's picked while young and tender in the early spring and cooked with bacon. When poke sallet isn't available, fresh spinach is prepared in the same way—and the resulting dish is given this rather long name. Although the recipe is quite simple, the bacon bits give the cooked spinach an incomparable flavor.

1 10-ounce package fresh
  spinach

4 slices bacon
⅛ teaspoon salt

Wash the spinach well and discard any tough stems and wilted leaves. Place in a large pot with just the water that clings to the leaves. Cook, covered, over medium heat until the spinach wilts, about 10 minutes. Drain well.

Meanwhile, cook the bacon in a skillet until crisp. Drain off all but 2 tablespoons bacon fat and cut the bacon into quarters. Add the spinach and salt. Cover and heat through.

Yield: 4 servings.

Stewed Tomato Casserole

❖

This is a longtime Southern favorite rarely found in other parts of the country, which is a pity, for it's marvelous with almost any meat dish. The casserole is a slightly tart, slightly sweet mixture of tomatoes that's nicely thickened with toasted bread crumbs. Any type of canned tomatoes can be used, but I have found that those packed in thick tomato puree require less cooking to achieve the proper consistency.

*1 28-ounce can tomatoes,
undrained and coarsely
chopped*
*2 tablespoons butter or
margarine*

⅓ cup sugar
*2 slices white bread, toasted
and crumbled*

Place the tomatoes, butter, and sugar in a saucepan and heat until the butter melts. Add the bread crumbs and continue simmering until most of the liquid is absorbed, about 15 minutes.

Turn the mixture into a greased 1½-quart round casserole and bake in a 350° oven until thick and bubbly, about 20 to 30 minutes.

Yield: 6 servings.

Fried Green Tomatoes

❖

This recipe will come in handy at the end of summer, when lots of green tomatoes are left unripened on the vine and anyone with a garden is wondering how to use up a bumper crop. It's marvelously easy and calls for only a few ingredients, but the flavor is unusual and deliciously hearty.

1 medium-sized green tomato *Pepper*
  per person *White cornmeal*
Salt *Bacon drippings*

Slice the tomatoes ¼ inch thick. Season with salt and pepper and then coat both cut sides with cornmeal.

In a large skillet, heat enough bacon drippings to coat the bottom of the pan and sauté the tomatoes until lightly browned on each side. It may be necessary to cook the tomatoes in batches, in which case keep the fried tomatoes warm in a low oven until all are cooked. Add more bacon drippings as necessary.

Skillet Corn with Bacon

❖

This creamed, bacon-flavored corn was a real favorite at Miss Mary's in the late summer when the corn harvest is at its peak.

3 slices thick-sliced bacon   *1½ teaspoons sugar*
4 ears corn   *¼ teaspoon salt*
½ cup water

Cook the bacon in a heavy skillet. (Do not use an iron skillet, as this may cause the corn to turn dark.) Remove the bacon and drain on paper towels. Crumble and reserve.

Remove the husks and silk from the corn. (This next step is optional because it is quite time-consuming, but it will result in a creamier dish: with a sharp knife, cut halfway through each kernel to release the milky liquid inside.) With a sharp knife, cut the kernels from the ears. Then, using the blunt side of the knife, scrape off any milky portions of the kernels that remain on the ear.

Drain off all but 2 tablespoons bacon fat from the skillet and heat remaining fat. Add the corn, water, sugar, and salt. Cook, stirring often, 15 to 20 minutes, or until the mixture has thickened and turned somewhat creamy.

Transfer to a serving dish and sprinkle with the reserved bacon.
Yield: 4 servings.

Mustard and Turnip Greens

❖

This classic Southern standby is marvelously satisfying on a cold day, especially when accompanied by wedges of Skillet Corn Bread (page 102).

In the South, it's traditional to serve some of the cooking liquid with the greens. This is called "pot liquor" and is used for moistening the accompanying chunks of corn bread.

2 ham hocks	1 dried red pepper (if
2 quarts water	unavailable, substitute
3 pounds mustard greens	½ teaspoon hot pepper
4 pounds turnip greens	sauce)
2 teaspoons sugar	4 hard-cooked eggs, halved

Place the ham hocks in a large saucepan with the water. Bring to a boil. Lower the heat and simmer, covered, 2 hours.

Meanwhile, cut the stems from the greens and discard. Tear the greens into large pieces and wash in warm, salted water until free of any dirt. Let drain in a colander.

Skim any fat from the ham-cooking liquid. Remove the hocks and cut the meat into bite-size pieces, discarding the skin and bones. Return the meat to the pot and add the sugar and red pepper. Add as many greens as will fit in the pot. Cover and cook until the greens are wilted. Repeat until all the greens are in the pot. Continue cooking, covered, about 1½ hours. Remove red pepper and drain before serving.

Garnish with eggs. Serve a cruet of distilled white vinegar on the side for additional seasoning.

Yield: 8 to 10 servings.

Scalloped Potatoes

❖

For those who have tasted only scalloped potatoes from a packaged mix, this dish will come as a delightful surprise. The meltingly tender potato slices are coated in a rich and cheesy cream
sauce. Browned and bubbly when it comes to the table, this dish
raises the humble spud to supreme gastronomic heights.

3 tablespoons butter
3 tablespoons flour
3 cups milk
1 teaspoon salt
⅛ teaspoon pepper
⅔ cup shredded Cheddar
  cheese

6 medium baking potatoes,
  peeled and thinly sliced
1 small onion, minced
  (about ¼ cup)

Melt the butter in a saucepan. Stir in the flour. Add the milk
and cook, stirring constantly, until the sauce comes to a boil and
has thickened slightly. Remove from the heat and stir in the salt,
pepper, and Cheddar cheese.

In a greased 2-quart casserole, layer half the potato slices.
Sprinkle with half the onion and cover with half the sauce. Repeat layers.

Bake the casserole, covered, in a 350° oven 1 hour. Remove
the cover and continue baking 30 minutes longer.

Yield: 6 servings.

Cheese-Topped Mashed Potatoes

❖

For mashed potato fans, here's a simple way to add spice to plain potatoes—just another example of Miss Mary's ingenuity when it comes to making ordinary favorites taste extraordinary.

6 *medium potatoes, peeled*
  and quartered
1 *tablespoon butter*
⅓ *cup milk*
½ *teaspoon salt*

⅛ *teaspoon pepper*
¼ *teaspoon celery seed*
1 *egg yolk*
½ *cup shredded Cheddar*
  cheese

Place the potatoes in a saucepan and cover with salted water. Cook, covered, until tender, about 20 to 30 minutes. Drain well.

Mash the potatoes with a fork, potato masher, or electric mixer and beat in all remaining ingredients except the cheese.

Turn the potatoes into a greased 1½-quart round casserole and sprinkle the cheese on top. Bake the potatoes in a 350° oven 10 minutes, until the cheese is melted. Serve at once.

Yield: 4 to 6 servings.

Note: Although fresh potatoes were always the rule in Mary Bobo's kitchen, if you're in a hurry, you may substitute instant mashed potato flakes. Simply use a 7-serving envelope and follow the directions on the package; just be sure to omit the milk and butter called for in the recipe.

April 10. Mr. R., Sion, Dance and myself planted Irish potatoes, popcorn, bunch beans, corn, beans, etc. this morning and then Sion went with Luther and Jack N. fishing. I have been busy today piecing quilts and doing all the necessary jobs about a home. There are so many things to see about now, since gardening and chicken raising are on hand. I have only 20 young chickens and the hogs are helping to eat them. Late this evening Eula and I went to Mrs. Sue H.'s and gathered a bucket of turnip salad.

Sue Dance Record's Diary, 1896.

Candied Sweet Potatoes

❖

In most parts of the country, sweet potatoes are reserved for holiday dinners. Not so in the South, however, where you're likely to be served this luscious vegetable as an accompaniment to just about any meal throughout the fall and winter. In the "Holiday Foods" chapter, there's a recipe for sweet potatoes that's a bit more elaborate, but this recipe is certainly appropriate for any holiday feast. Moreover it takes just a few minutes to fix and is virtually foolproof.

4 sweet potatoes
¼ cup granulated sugar
¼ cup light or dark brown
  sugar

2 tablespoons butter
¼ cup water

Place the sweet potatoes in a saucepan and cover with plenty of water. Bring the water to a boil. Cover the pot and cook the potatoes until just tender, about 30 minutes. Drain. When cool enough to handle, peel the potatoes and cut into ½-inch slices.

Place the sliced potatoes in a greased 8-inch-square baking pan and sprinkle with the sugars. Dot with the butter and pour the water over all.

Bake the potatoes in a 375° oven about 30 minutes, or until the sugars have formed a thick syrup. Baste potatoes occasionally while baking.

Yield: 4 servings.

Hoppin' John

❖

Although this traditional Southern dish is always eaten on New Year's Day to bring good luck in the year ahead—and legend has it that if you dare to eat Hoppin' John at any other time of year, it will bring on bad luck, no one I asked was able to supply the origin of its unusual name.

*1 pound dried black-eyed peas,
  washed and picked over
8½ cups water, divided
½ pound smoked hog jowl or
  ham hock
1 onion, sliced*

*1 pod hot red pepper (or
  substitute ½ teaspoon hot
  pepper sauce)
¼ teaspoon salt
1 cup rice*

Place the peas in a large pot and add 6 cups water. Let soak overnight.

The next day, add the hog jowl or ham hock, onion, and red pepper to the peas. Bring to a boil. Then reduce the heat and cook, covered, until the peas and meat are tender, about 1¼ hours. Remove from the heat. Remove pepper pod.

In another saucepan, heat the remaining 2½ cups water with the salt. When it comes to a boil, add the rice. Lower the heat and cook, covered, until the rice is tender and all liquid has been absorbed, about 20 minutes.

Meanwhile, remove any skin and bones from the jowl or hock and cut the meat into small pieces. Return the meat to the pot.

Add the rice to the pot with the peas and heat through.
Yield: 10 servings.

Simmered Dried Beans

❖

Here's a hearty side dish that's perfect for the winter months when fresh vegetables are scarce. The original Tennessee recipe calls for "middling meat," which is salt-cured bacon. Since this is not readily available in most parts of the country, I've substituted ordinary sugar-cured bacon. However, if you do have access to the real thing, by all means use it to make an authentic version of this marvelously easy-to-fix bean dish.

1 cup dried beans	*¼ pound middling meat or*
Water for soaking beans	*bacon (about 5 slices)*
1½ cups additional water	*¼ teaspoon salt*

Wash the beans and soak overnight in enough water to cover by about 2 extra inches.

The next day, pour off this water. Place the beans, the 1½ cups fresh water, meat and salt in a saucepan. Bring to a boil. Then lower the heat and simmer, uncovered, 45 minutes to 1 hour, or until the beans are tender and most of the liquid has evaporated. Cut the meat or bacon into small pieces and serve with the beans.

Yield: 4 servings.

Note: Many different types of dried beans may be used for this recipe—small white beans (often called pea beans), pinto beans, black-eyed peas, crowder peas, butter beans, or lima beans.

Baked Macaroni and Cheese

❖

This must be one of the simplest of all macaroni and cheese dishes to put together—just a few ingredients layered in a casserole and then baked—but, for a dish that requires so little effort, the results are marvelous. The casserole comes to the table with a delightfully crisp, brown topping and, underneath, plenty of melted Cheddar cheese and tender macaroni.

At Miss Mary's, this is just one of several starch dishes that accompany the main course. You may use it to perk up any plain meat or poultry dish—or fix it as a quick and easy Sunday night supper.

2 cups elbow macaroni, cooked in boiling salted water until tender, then drained
Black pepper, to taste

2 cups shredded Cheddar cheese
2 cups crushed saltine crackers
2½ cups milk

In a round, greased 2-quart casserole, place one-fourth of the macaroni. Season lightly with pepper. Top with one-fourth of the cheese, then one-fourth of the cracker crumbs. Repeat layers until all ingredients are used. Slowly pour the milk over the top.

Bake the casserole, uncovered, in a 350° oven 50 minutes, or until browned on top.

Yield: 6 servings.

Hominy Casserole

❖

Hominy is corn that has been specially treated so that the kernels puff up dramatically. When dried and ground, hominy becomes grits. Hominy is most often served heated from the can and seasoned with salt and pepper and a pat of butter. But for special meals try this luscious casserole of hominy layered with chili peppers, sour cream, and Monterey Jack cheese.

1 29-ounce can hominy,
* drained*
1 4-ounce can green chili
* peppers, finely chopped*
½ cup sour cream

Salt
¼ cup light or heavy cream
¾ cup shredded Monterey
* Jack cheese*

Grease a 1½-quart round casserole and place one-fourth of the hominy in it. Sprinkle with one-fourth of the chili peppers and dot with one-fourth of the sour cream. Season lightly with salt. Repeat these layers three more times.

Pour the cream over the casserole and sprinkle with the cheese. Bake the casserole in a 350° oven 30 minutes.

Yield: 6 servings.

Note: Hominy is found in the canned vegetable section of the supermarket. In some parts of the country, however, it's difficult to locate. If you can't find it but would like to sample this delicious dish, substitute a 24-ounce package of frozen corn kernels, defrosted. It won't taste quite the same, but you're certain to find it mighty flavorful.

Garlic. Garlic eliminates every kind of intestinal parasite, and cures more diseases than the medical profession has invented names for. It is superior in every way to any member of the onion family and is eaten in every way that onions are. Boiled in March, it will make the best onion stew you ever tasted.

I have cured my wife of pleurisy, that medico-invented disease, by administering a tea made from garlic every time she coughs. Formerly she could not sleep, for coughing. So marvelous is this plant that, two weeks after using the garlic tea, she sleeps eight or more hours each night. I make the tea from whatever seasonal stage of the plant is available (in summer from the seeds) by steeping it in hot water several hours, but not permitting the water to come to a boil. Whenever she shows the first symptom of a coughing fit, my wife drinks a little of this cold—we keep a jar of it in the refrigerator. The coughing stops as if by magic. Also the tea has stopped her from snoring. For the forty years I have been sleeping with her, she was the loudest snorer I ever heard.

On Man and the Good Life. Leaves from the Notebook of Emmett Gowen.

84

Garlic Cheese Grits

❖

For those unfamiliar with Southern cooking, grits are ground from hominy, which is the corn kernel relieved of its hull and germ and then soaked in wood ash lye. The end result tastes very much like cornmeal but has a milder flavor and lighter texture. Grits are served for breakfast throughout the South as an accompaniment to eggs, ham, sausage, or bacon.

Miss Mary's grits, served with dinner as a rich starch, are enhanced with Cheddar cheese and the heady aroma of garlic and then baked until deliciously browned.

4 cups water
1 clove garlic, pressed
½ teaspoon salt
⅛ teaspoon pepper
1 cup quick-cooking grits
(found in the cereal section
of the supermarket)

2 tablespoons butter or
    margarine
1¼ cups shredded Cheddar
    cheese, divided
2 eggs, beaten
½ cup milk

In a large saucepan, bring the water to a boil, adding the garlic, salt, and pepper. Gradually stir in the grits. Lower the heat and simmer, stirring occasionally, 5 minutes.

Remove the pan from the heat and stir in the butter and 1 cup Cheddar cheese until the butter melts. Mix the eggs with the milk and stir thoroughly into the grits.

Turn the grits into a greased 2-quart round casserole. Sprinkle with the remaining ¼ cup cheese. Bake in a 350° oven 1 hour, or until set and browned.

Yield: 4 to 6 servings.

Baked Apples

❖

Although the ingredients may be the same, Miss Mary's Baked Apples are nothing like the whole baked apples eaten in most parts of the country. Rather, these are sliced and candied, so they are very tender and sweet. They are served as a relish—as one would serve ordinary commercial spiced apple rings—to accompany plain meats or poultry.

*4 cups (about 1½ pounds)
    cooking apples, peeled,
    cored, and thickly sliced
2 tablespoons butter or
    margarine*

*3 cups sugar
½ teaspoon nutmeg*

Place all ingredients in a saucepan and cook, stirring occasionally, until the butter melts and the sugar dissolves.

Turn the mixture into a greased 8-inch-square baking dish. Bake the apples in a 375° oven 30 minutes, or until the apples are tender and the sauce bubbly. Serve warm.

Yield: 4 servings.

Cabbage Slaw

❖

You'd be a lot more likely to find Cabbage Slaw on Miss Mary's table than the leafy green salads usually served in other parts of the country. It is a very fitting accompaniment to Fried Chicken (page 45), Pepper Meat Loaf (page 36), and barbecued foods, and Mary Bobo's version is pleasantly crisp, with a delicious sweet-and-sour dressing that's sparked with grated onion, mustard, and celery seed.

*1 medium head cabbage,
    grated
1 medium onion, grated
½ cup cider vinegar
½ cup sugar*

*2½ tablespoons vegetable oil
1½ tablespoons prepared
    mustard
1½ teaspoons salt
½ teaspoon celery seed*

Put the cabbage and onion in a large bowl.

In a small saucepan, heat the remaining ingredients to boiling, stirring to blend in the sugar and mustard. Pour over the cabbage and toss well.

Refrigerate several hours before serving. The slaw will keep well for about a week.

Yield: about 6 cups, or 8 to 10 servings.

Wilted Lettuce

❖

This very special dish at Miss Mary's was always served in the spring when the lettuce and green onions in her garden were first coming up and tender. The salad itself is fresh and crisp, but once the hot, smoky bacon dressing is poured over the greens, the leaves become a bit "wilted" and even more tender.

Salad

1 head romaine lettuce, or
    2 heads Boston or other
    leafy lettuce, or 1 10-ounce
    package fresh spinach,
    washed, dried, and torn into
    bite-size pieces

6 radishes, thinly sliced
4 green onions, sliced
2 hard-cooked eggs, minced

Dressing

5 slices bacon
2 tablespoons red wine
    vinegar
1 tablespoon freshly squeezed
    lemon juice

1 teaspoon sugar
½ teaspoon freshly ground
    black pepper

Place the greens, radishes, and green onions in a salad bowl.

Cook the bacon in a skillet until browned. Remove the bacon, crumble, and set aside. Add the vinegar, lemon juice, sugar, and pepper to the skillet and bring to a boil, stirring.

Pour the hot dressing over the lettuce and toss well. Garnish with the egg and bacon. Serve immediately.

Yield: 6 servings.

Country Potato Salad

❖

Diced hard-cooked eggs, sweet pickles, and grated onion add zip to this perennial favorite at Miss Mary's—and practically everywhere else in the country, for that matter.

4 medium potatoes, peeled
and quartered
3 hard-cooked eggs
½ cup diced sweet cucumber
pickles ("bread and butter"
pickles)

1 tablespoon grated onion
¼ teaspoon salt
⅛ teaspoon pepper
2 to 4 tablespoons mayonnaise,
or to taste

Place the potatoes in a saucepan and cover with water. Bring to a boil and cook until tender, about 15 minutes. Drain and dice.

Finely dice 2 of the hard-cooked eggs and slice the third.

Toss the potatoes with the diced eggs and all remaining ingredients. Place in a serving bowl and garnish with the sliced egg. Chill until ready to serve.

Yield: 4 servings.

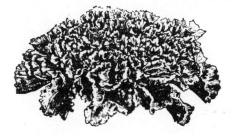

Fresh Tomato Aspic

❖

Fresh green onions, tomatoes, and cucumbers lend a delightful garden taste to this most flavorful aspic, made with chicken broth and seasoned with dill, lemon juice, and hot pepper sauce. It's a wonderful side dish on a hot summer day.

1 envelope unflavored gelatin
1 cup chicken broth, at room
*   temperature*
½ cup tomato juice
1 tablespoon freshly squeezed
*   lemon juice*
1 teaspoon dried dillweed
¼ teaspoon hot pepper sauce

2 tablespoons finely minced
*   green onion*
1 cup peeled, seeded, and
*   chopped tomatoes*
½ cup peeled, seeded, and
*   chopped cucumber*
Cottage cheese

Soften the gelatin in the chicken broth. Then heat over medium heat, stirring until the gelatin dissolves. Remove from the heat and stir in the tomato juice, lemon juice, dill, and hot pepper sauce. Chill until syrupy.

Fold the green onion, tomatoes, and cucumber into the chilled gelatin mixture. Turn the mixture into an 8-inch-square pan or 1-quart mold and chill until firm. Serve with a small scoop of cottage cheese on each portion.

Yield: 6 servings.

Date Waldorf Salad

❖

Here's a fancied-up version of the traditional Waldorf Salad, that wonderful mixture of apples, celery, and mayonnaise that's so delicious on a crisp fall day.

½ cup diced celery
2 cups diced, unpeeled red
  apples

½ cup chopped, pitted dates
½ cup broken pecans
½ cup mayonnaise, or to taste

In a bowl, mix together the celery, apples, dates, and nuts. Toss with the mayonnaise and chill well.

  Yield: 6 servings.

Honey. Nearly all we eat and most of what we drink we raise right here. Three bee gums gave us 150 pounds of honey last year, almost enough to last until now, when new honey is in rapid making. We use no sugar. The washing of the hive frames and the combs produces honey-water, which, added to fruit juices, last year made thirty to forty gallons of fruited mead. Should that spoil, there would result vinegar the purity of which I know, but I have not learned how to make it spoil. We are always short of vinegar.

On Man and the Good Life. Leaves from the Notebook of Emmett Gowen.

Molded Orange–Pineapple Salad

❖

In the South, sweet gelatin salads like this one are often served as an accompaniment to the main course. This salad would also make a delicious light dessert, although you'd have been unlikely to find it served as the meal's finale at Miss Mary's.

1 large (6-ounce) package
    orange-flavored gelatin
    dessert
2 cups boiling water
2 cups cold water
1 11-ounce can mandarin
    oranges, drained

1 8-ounce can crushed
    pineapple, drained
1 cup cottage cheese
½ cup coarsely chopped
    pecans
1 cup heavy (whipping)
    cream, whipped until stiff

Dissolve the gelatin in the boiling water. Add the cold water. Mix in the fruits, cottage cheese, and pecans. Fold in the whipped cream gently but thoroughly.

Pour the mixture into an 8-cup gelatin mold or a large rectangular baking pan. Chill until set. Stir the mixture a few times while chilling to prevent the heavier ingredients from settling to the bottom.

To serve, unmold onto a lettuce-lined plate or cut into squares and serve on individual lettuce-lined plates. (At Mary Bobo's, each serving was topped with a dollop of mayonnaise.)

Yield: 10 to 12 servings.

Cream Cheese–Pineapple Salad

❖

Gelatin salads, or congealed salads as they're called in Tennessee, are mighty popular around Lynchburg. In summer, a gelatin salad is refreshingly light and cool; in the winter, when salad greens are harder to come by, recipes like this one and those that follow are very convenient. This salad is not too sweet and the nuts and bits of celery give it a delightful crisp texture.

1 3-ounce package lemon gelatin
1 cup boiling water
1 20-ounce can crushed pineapple, packed in juice
1 3-ounce package cream cheese, softened
1 4-ounce jar pimientos, drained and chopped
½ cup diced celery
¾ cup chopped pecans
½ pint heavy (whipping) cream, whipped until stiff

Dissolve the gelatin in the boiling water. Drain the pineapple and add enough water to the liquid to make 1 cup. Stir into the gelatin.

In a large bowl, cream the cream cheese. Beat in the gelatin. Stir in the pineapple, pimientos, celery, and pecans. Fold in the whipped cream gently.

Pour the mixture into an 8-cup gelatin mold or a large rectangular pan. Chill well. To serve, unmold or cut into squares.

Yield: 8 servings.

Orange Sherbet Salad

❖

Orange sherbet, mandarin orange segments, crushed pineapple, and miniature marshmallows go into a salad that goes well with simple meat and poultry dishes and can also be enjoyed as a light and refreshing dessert.

1 3-ounce package orange gelatin
1 cup boiling water
1 cup orange sherbet
1 8-ounce can crushed pineapple, undrained (preferably juice-packed)

1 11-ounce can mandarin oranges, drained
½ cup miniature marshmallows

Dissolve the gelatin in the boiling water. Add the sherbet and stir until dissolved. Add the remaining ingredients and mix well.

Turn the mixture into a 1-quart mold or bowl and chill until set.

Yield: 6 servings.

Buttermilk Salad

❖

The buttermilk gives the salad a refreshing tart quality that contrasts well with the sweet gelatin. The salad may be made with any flavored gelatin; raspberry is particularly good and lends a delicate pink color.

1 3-ounce package flavored
  gelatin
¾ cup boiling water
1 8-ounce can crushed
  pineapple, preferably
  juice-packed, undrained

1 cup buttermilk
½ cup heavy (whipping)
  cream, whipped

Dissolve the gelatin in the boiling water. Stir in the pineapple, then the buttermilk. Fold in the whipped cream.

  Turn the mixture into a 1-quart mold and chill until set.

  Yield: 6 servings.

Blueberry Gelatin Mold

❖

The fresh creaminess of the topping gives this salad the refreshing taste of fresh blueberries and cream.

Gelatin

1 3-ounce package raspberry
  gelatin
1 3-ounce package black
  cherry gelatin
2 cups boiling water
1 cup cold water

1 20-ounce can juice-packed
  crushed pineapple, drained
  and juice reserved
1 21-ounce can blueberry pie
  filling

Topping

1 3-ounce package cream
  cheese, softened

1 cup sour cream
½ cup sugar

Dissolve the gelatin in the boiling water. Stir in the cold water and the juice from the pineapple. Stir in the blueberry pie filling. Chill until syrupy and then stir in the pineapple. Chill until firm.

In a small bowl, cream together the topping ingredients. Spread over the gelatin and chill until ready to serve.

Yield: 10 servings.

Frozen Cherry Salad

❖

At Miss Mary's, this frozen salad was served garnished with a dollop of mayonnaise and a fresh cherry. Although it is quite sweet—almost like ice cream, in fact—it is particularly refreshing on a hot summer day. It takes only minutes to prepare and, as it is served frozen, offers the advantage of advance preparation.

1 14-ounce can sweetened
  condensed milk (not
  evaporated milk)
¼ cup freshly squeezed lemon
  juice
1 21-ounce can cherry pie
  filling

1 8-ounce can crushed
  pineapple, drained
2 ripe bananas, sliced
½ cup coarsely chopped
  pecans
1 cup heavy (whipping)
  cream, whipped until stiff

In a large bowl, stir together the sweetened condensed milk and lemon juice. This will thicken the milk somewhat. Stir in the cherry pie filling, pineapple, bananas, and pecans. Fold in the whipped cream.

You may freeze the mixture in the bowl and serve it scooped out into small bowls. Or you may transfer it to a large rectangular pan for freezing and serve it cut into squares.

Yield: 10 servings.

Breads & Rolls

In ONE FORM or another, hot corn breads, biscuits, or yeast rolls were served at Miss Mary's just about every day. In fact, it's probably safe to say that her guests would have been mighty disappointed not to find a pan of corn bread or a basket full of hot-from-the-oven biscuits on the table when they sat down for the noon meal.

The biscuits might have been the traditional "quick" variety, leavened with baking powder, or they might have been made from an exceptionally light and flaky yeast dough. Either way, they were generally served with meat in gravy. If the meat had no gravy, the biscuits would be split and buttered and often filled with a thin slice of country ham or sausage as well.

As elsewhere in the South, the cooks at Miss Mary's baked their corn breads in a cast-iron skillet, which assures a deliciously crisp crust. These breads were served right from the oven while the fragrant steam was still escaping. Another type of skillet corn bread is the quickly made Hoe Cake, a sort of cross between the traditional baked variety and a pancake.

Most of the breads and rolls in this chapter take only a few minutes to put together, and all will add immeasurably to the good flavor of your meals, as they did to Mary Bobo's.

February 14. This morning early we went to washing out some things and Mr. R. began to make preparation to have a hog killed. Mr. Miles B. killed the hog free of charge. I had so many tasks running to and fro that I was glad when Eula announced dinner and gladder still to sit by the fire after dinner was over. Mrs. B. came over to get a supply of scraps to put in her gizzard quilt. Mary went out trying to get some money in her Missionary Box.

Sue Dance Record's Diary, 1896.

Corn Muffins

❖

Buttermilk in the batter makes these about the lightest and freshest-tasting corn muffins you'll ever sample. Serve them hot from the oven with plenty of butter.

1 cup cornmeal, preferably white
1 cup flour
2 tablespoons sugar
1½ teaspoons salt
½ teaspoon baking soda
2 tablespoons butter or margarine, melted

2 eggs, beaten
1½ cups buttermilk (or make "soured" milk: place 1½ tablespoons distilled white vinegar in a measuring cup and fill to the 1½-cup mark with milk; stir)

In a bowl, stir together the dry ingredients. In another bowl, stir together the remaining ingredients. Add to the dry ingredients and stir just until moistened.

Spoon the batter into well-greased muffin cups, filling them a little more than three-fourths full. Bake the muffins in a 425° oven about 25 minutes, or until they are lightly browned. Remove from the tins to a rack.

Yield: about 1 dozen muffins.

Skillet Corn Bread

❖

Miss Mary's is the traditional Southern corn bread, baked in a heavy cast-iron skillet to ensure a crisp, golden crust. It should be served warm right from the oven, with plenty of butter. Any leftover bread can be turned into the marvelous Corn Bread Dressing casserole (see page 180).

*2 tablespoons lard or
   vegetable oil
2 cups cornmeal, preferably
   white
1 teaspoon baking soda
½ teaspoon salt
2 eggs, beaten with a fork*

*1 cup buttermilk (you may
   substitute "soured" milk:
   place 1 tablespoon distilled
   white vinegar in a measuring cup and fill to the 1-cup
   mark with milk; stir)*

Turn the oven on to 350° to preheat. Place lard or oil in an 8-inch or 9-inch heavy cast-iron skillet and place in the oven while you are preparing the batter.

In a bowl, stir together the cornmeal, baking soda, and salt. In another bowl, mix together the eggs and buttermilk. Add to the dry ingredients, mixing with a spoon until the dry ingredients are just moistened; do not overmix.

Remove the skillet from the oven. Tilt the pan to grease the bottom and sides and pour the hot lard or oil into the batter. Stir until it is incorporated.

Turn the batter into the hot skillet. Place in the 350° oven 20 to 25 minutes, or until a toothpick inserted in the bread comes out clean.

Yield: 8 to 10 servings.

Note: A cast-iron skillet is best for baking corn bread. Naturally, it must have an ovenproof handle. If you lack this utensil, you may bake the bread in an 8-inch-square baking pan, but the crust will not be quite so crisp.

In the South it is traditional to use white cornmeal, although you can certainly substitute the yellow variety with equally delicious results. Try to buy cornmeal that hasn't been degerminated, because the corn germ, like wheat germ, adds wholesome flavor.

Hoe Cakes

❖

Hoe Cakes, so named because they were originally cooked on the ends of hoes over an open fire, date back to Colonial days and are one of the few recipes shared by both North and South. The main difference is that while most parts of the country no longer prepare these pancakelike morsels, they are still very popular in the South. They're remarkably quick to fix, as they call for only three ingredients: cornmeal, salt, and water.

1½ cups cornmeal, preferably   *2¼ cups boiling water*
   white   *Oil for skillet*
½ teaspoon salt

Stir together the cornmeal and salt and then stir in the water.

Heat a griddle or large skillet and oil it lightly. Drop the batter by tablespoons onto the skillet. Cook until browned on one side. Turn and brown the other side. Serve immediately, spread with butter.

Yield: about 20 hoe cakes, serving about 4 people.

Corn Light Bread

❖

Here's another skillet corn bread, this one made light and airy with yeast. The bread has the advantages of ordinary yeast breads without the bother of kneading the dough. Just mix, let rise for half an hour, and bake. At Miss Mary's, melted butter was poured over the baked bread as soon as it emerged from the oven, which produces a luscious moistness and rich buttery flavor. If you prefer, though, you may serve the bread with pats of butter at the table.

½ stick (¼ cup) butter
2 cups cornmeal, preferably
   white
1 cup flour
½ teaspoon salt
¼ cup sugar
1 teaspoon baking powder
½ teaspoon baking soda
1 package (2½ teaspoons)
   active dry yeast
2½ cups buttermilk, heated
   to lukewarm

Place the butter in a heavy cast-iron skillet with an ovenproof handle and melt over low heat. Rotate the skillet slightly to grease the sides.

In a mixing bowl, stir together the cornmeal, flour, salt, sugar, baking powder, baking soda, and yeast. Add the buttermilk and stir until well mixed. Turn into the skillet.

Cover the skillet and let the batter rise in a warm, draft-free spot for 30 minutes.

Bake the bread, uncovered, in a 350° oven 30 minutes, or until a toothpick inserted in the center comes out clean. Serve hot.

Yield: 10 servings.

"Riz" Biscuits

❖

Southern cooks have long been renowned for their exceptionally light biscuits. These morsels, also dubbed "angel biscuits," are among the lightest and most delicate you'll ever encounter.

1 package (2½ teaspoons)
   active dry yeast
1 cup warm buttermilk (or
   use 1 tablespoon distilled
   white vinegar plus enough
   warm milk to equal 1 cup)
½ teaspoon baking soda

2½ cups flour
2 tablespoons sugar
½ teaspoon salt
½ cup lard or solid vegetable
   shortening
About 2 tablespoons melted
   butter or margarine

In a bowl, dissolve the yeast in the warm buttermilk. Stir in the baking soda.

In a large bowl, stir together the flour, sugar, and salt. Cut in the lard or shortening with a pastry cutter or two knives until the mixture is like coarse meal. Add yeast mixture and stir well.

Turn the dough out onto a floured surface and roll out to about ½-inch thick. Brush with the melted butter or margarine. Cut into 2- to 2½-inch rounds with a biscuit cutter and place almost touching, buttered side down, on a greased baking sheet. Brush the tops with butter. Cover lightly with plastic wrap and let rise in a warm, draft-free spot for 1 hour.

Bake the biscuits in a 425° oven until lightly browned, about 25 minutes. Serve immediately with butter or gravy.

Yield: about 20 biscuits.

Note: Despite the yeast, no kneading is involved. However, there is a wait between mixing and eating because the biscuits have to rise.

Buttermilk Biscuits

❖

These light, flaky biscuits make almost any meal more special. At Miss Mary's the biscuits were served hot from the oven with plenty of butter. Or, if she was serving fried chicken, she would fix some gravy to accompany the biscuits. In the old days, when breakfast was served at the boardinghouse, a plateful of hot biscuits, served with jams, appeared at every morning meal.

2 cups flour
2 teaspoons baking powder
½ teaspoon baking soda
½ teaspoon salt
¼ cup lard or solid vegetable
  shortening

¾ cup buttermilk (or
  substitute "soured" milk:
  place 2 teaspoons distilled
  white vinegar in a measur-
  ing cup and fill to the
  ¾-cup mark with milk;
  stir)

In a mixing bowl, stir together the flour, baking powder, baking soda, and salt. With a pastry cutter or two knives, cut in the lard or shortening until the mixture is in very fine crumbs. Stir in the buttermilk and knead for about 30 seconds, or until the dough is no longer sticky. Don't overknead, as this will make the biscuits tough.

Roll out the dough to a little less than ½-inch thick and cut into rounds with a 2-inch cutter. Place on a greased baking sheet.

Bake the biscuits in a 450° oven about 15 minutes, or until golden brown. Serve immediately.

Yield: about 16 biscuits.

Note: To make gravy to serve with biscuits: Place 2 table-spoons pan drippings from a beef roast in a small saucepan. Stir in 2 tablespoons flour and cook, stirring, for 1 minute. Add 1 cup juices from roast or water and cook, stirring, until the mixture comes to a boil and thickens. Yield: 1 cup.

January 18. Nineteen years ago tonight at half past six o'clock Bro. Collier pronounced Mr. R. and I husband and wife. It seems that it has not been more than half so long, yet circumstances or rather facts prove it to be that way. Pa and Ma had a large circle of relatives and friends to witness our marriage and partake of the wedding feast.

Sue Dance Record's Diary, 1896.

Hot Rolls

❖

It's the aroma of rolls like these that helps create the sense of nostalgia that comes over visitors to Miss Mary's boardinghouse. Served hot from the oven with plenty of butter, these pan rolls are golden brown on the outside, light and fluffy within.

*½ cup lard or solid vegetable
 shortening
½ cup boiling water
¼ cup sugar
1 teaspoon salt*

*1 package (2½ teaspoons)
 active dry yeast, dissolved
 in ½ cup lukewarm water
1 egg
About 3½ cups flour*

Place the lard or shortening in a large mixing bowl and pour the boiling water over it. Stir until the shortening has melted. Stir in the sugar, salt, yeast mixture, and egg. Add the flour gradually, beating it in well.

When the dough is stiff, turn it out onto a floured surface and knead until smooth, elastic, and no longer sticky, continuing to add more flour as necessary. Break off pieces of dough large enough to shape into 2½-inch-diameter balls. Place the balls side by side, nearly touching, in a greased 9-inch-square pan (or use an 8-inch by 12-inch rectangular pan).

Cover the dough with plastic wrap and let sit in a warm, draft-free spot until the rolls have doubled in size, about 1 hour.

Bake the rolls in a 425° oven until they are golden brown, about 25 minutes. Serve warm.

Yield: about 1 dozen rolls.

Note: Unlike most yeast breads, these rolls require only one rising and so can be whipped up quickly.

Buttermilk Bread

❖

Buttermilk lends fine texture and fresh flavor to this bread.

1 package (2½ teaspoons)	*1 teaspoon baking soda*
active dry yeast	*2 cups buttermilk*
½ cup warm water	*1 stick (½ cup) butter*
⅓ cup sugar	*1 egg*
2 teaspoons salt	*7 to 8 cups flour*

In a large bowl, dissolve the yeast in the warm water. Add the sugar, salt, and baking soda.

In a saucepan, heat the buttermilk with the butter until the buttermilk is quite warm to the touch (the butter need not melt completely). Add to the yeast mixture, along with the egg and 1 cup flour. Beat well. Stir in enough additional flour, about 1 cup at a time, to make a firm dough.

Turn the dough out onto a floured board or counter and knead, adding more flour as necessary, until the dough is stiff, elastic, and no longer sticky. Place the dough in a greased bowl and rotate it so the greased side faces up. Cover the bowl with plastic wrap and let sit in a warm, draft-free spot until the dough has doubled in bulk, about 1½ hours.

Turn the dough out onto a floured surface and knead briefly. Divide in half and shape each half into a loaf. Place each in a greased 9 by 5-inch loaf pan. Cover and let rise until doubled, about 1 hour.

Place the loaves in a 400° oven and let bake 10 minutes. Lower the heat to 350° and bake about 35 minutes longer, or until the loaves are golden brown. Remove loaves from pans and let cool on a rack before slicing.

Yield: 2 loaves.

Banana–Pecan Bread

❖

This recipe was contributed by Mrs. Elizabeth Cobble, a retired teacher and presently the Moore County historian, who hosts one of the tables at the Bobo House each day. According to Mrs. Cobble, the bread improves if the banana flavor is allowed to mellow a bit. Either let the loaf sit, well wrapped, at room temperature for a day or in the freezer for a week. A slightly sweet bread, it goes well with simple meat and poultry dishes.

1 stick (½ cup) butter, softened
1 cup sugar
2 eggs
1 teaspoon vanilla extract

3 large or 3½ small very ripe bananas, mashed
2 cups flour
2 teaspoons baking powder
1 cup coarsely chopped pecans

In a large bowl, cream the butter with the sugar. Beat in the eggs, vanilla, and bananas.

In another bowl, stir together the flour and baking powder. Beat into the banana mixture, just until the dry ingredients are moistened. Stir in the pecans.

Turn the batter into a greased and floured 9 by 5-inch loaf pan. Bake the bread in a 325° oven 1 hour, 20 minutes, or until a toothpick inserted in the center comes out clean. Let cool on a rack.

Yield: 1 loaf, or about 10 slices.

Raisin and Nut Loaf

❖

Brown sugar and a touch of cocoa in the batter give this bread a rich, dark color and delightful aroma. This sweet bread is chock-full of nuts and raisins and, like others of its type, is best served with simple meat and poultry dishes.

2 cups raisins
1 teaspoon baking soda
2 cups boiling water
1 stick (½ cup) butter,
  softened
1½ cups light or dark brown
  sugar

2 eggs
3½ cups flour
2 tablespoons cocoa, sifted if
  lumpy
⅛ teaspoon salt
1 cup coarsely chopped
  walnuts

Place raisins in a bowl and sprinkle with baking soda. Add boiling water and stir. Let cool while preparing batter.

In a large bowl, cream the butter with the brown sugar. Beat in the eggs. In another bowl, stir together the flour, cocoa, and salt. Beat into the creamed mixture, along with the raisins and liquid in the bowl. Stir in the nuts.

Turn the batter into a greased and floured 5 by 9-inch loaf pan. Bake the bread in a 350° oven 1 hour, 20 minutes, or until a toothpick inserted in the center comes out clean. Transfer to a rack to cool. Let cool thoroughly before slicing.

Yield: 1 large loaf, or about 12 to 14 slices.

Honeyed Prune Bread

❖

This dense, dark loaf is filled with moist prunes and has a lovely honey flavor. It's delicious with poultry dishes or as a snack between meals.

1 teaspoon baking soda
1½ cups chopped dried
  prunes
1 cup boiling water
2 eggs
½ cup sugar
½ cup honey

½ stick (¼ cup) butter,
  melted
1 teaspoon vanilla extract
2¼ cups flour
1 cup coarsely chopped
  walnuts

Sprinkle the baking soda over the prunes in a bowl. Add the boiling water and stir. Let sit while preparing the batter.

Beat the eggs in a large bowl. Gradually beat in the sugar. The mixture should be thick and pale. Beat in the honey, melted butter, and vanilla. Add the flour and prunes, along with their liquid, and stir until well mixed. Stir in the walnuts.

Turn the batter into a greased and floured 5 by 9-inch loaf pan. Bake the bread in a 350° oven 1¼ hours, or until a toothpick inserted in the center comes out clean. Transfer to a rack to cool. Let cool thoroughly before slicing.

Yield: 1 loaf, or about 10 slices.

Pies & Other Desserts

DESSERTS are the crowning glory of the Southern kitchen and therefore deserve a prominent chapter in any book devoted to this cuisine. Miss Mary's kitchen was no exception. A typical noontime meal consisted of nearly a dozen different dishes, so diners were far from hungry when dessert was served, but no amount of fried chicken, hot biscuits, or Garlic Cheese Grits could diminish the anticipation of the final course.

Desserts at Miss Mary's, as elsewhere in Tennessee, weren't affected by diet consciousness. Rather, they were rich with butter and eggs and contained enough sugar to satisfy any sweet tooth. For the most part, these are desserts that were developed generations ago, and their hearty, traditional character is part of what makes them so very appealing still.

Pies form the mainstay of Southern desserts. At Miss Mary's you could find Fresh Peach Cobbler in the summer, Pumpkin Custard Pie during the holidays, and Glazed Strawberry Pie in the spring. But you would also have the opportunity to sample some regional specialties that you may never even have heard of—delectable favorites like refreshing Buttermilk Pie, ultrarich Chess Pie, or Caramel Meringue Pie with its creamy, puddinglike filling.

In addition to pies, Miss Mary served a range of other desserts —classic Strawberry Shortcake with real shortcakes (biscuits that are extra sweet and rich), delicate Glazed Apricot Cake, and

Crustless Fudge Pie, like a rich chocolate brownie that's topped with a scoop of ice cream.

The recipes in this chapter will help you understand why an opportunity to dine at Miss Mary's table was always coveted.

Pie Pastry

❖

Miss Mary served such a wide variety of pies that it's necessary to master the art of pastry-making in order to duplicate her fine desserts. Fortunately, it's relatively easy to make a piecrust that's tender and flaky if you observe a few simple rules:

- Handle the dough as little as possible, as overworking it produces a tough crust.
- Incorporate the shortening into the flour very thoroughly. This is most easily done with the steel blade of a food processor, but you may use a pastry blender or two knives.
- Use ice water in the dough, and add only enough to hold the dough together. Too much water and the dough becomes soggy. Even if you own a food processor, use a fork to blend in the water because the action of the food processor blade, used just a few seconds longer than necessary, can overwork the dough.
- If you have the time, chill the dough before rolling it out. This allows the flour to "rest" and produces a tenderer crust that's also easier to handle.

Note: Miss Mary used lard or solid shortening in her crusts. This produces a lighter, flakier crust than one made with butter or margarine. The latter ingredients, though, make for a finer flavor. One option is to use half lard or shortening and half butter or margarine.

For a 1-crust pie

1 cup flour
½ teaspoon salt
Pinch sugar
⅓ cup lard, shortening or chilled butter or margarine, or a combination

1½ to 2½ tablespoons ice water

For a 2-crust pie

2 cups flour
1 teaspoon salt
⅛ teaspoon sugar

⅔ cup lard, shortening or chilled butter or margarine, or a combination
3 to 5 tablespoons ice water

In a bowl, stir together the flour, salt, and sugar. With a pastry blender or two knives, cut in the lard, shortening, butter, or margarine until the fat is so fine that you almost cannot see it (this step may also be done with a food processor; transfer to a mixing bowl when completed).

Add the ice water gradually and blend it in with a fork. Use only enough water so the dough barely holds together.

If desired, chill the dough, wrapped in plastic wrap, for 1 hour.

Glazed Strawberry Pie

❖

This was a favorite springtime dessert at Miss Mary's. What's more, it's a snap to fix.

*Recipe for 1-crust pastry
  (page 115)*
2 cups water
*1 3-ounce box strawberry
  gelatin*
*1 tablespoon butter or
  margarine*
1½ teaspoons flour

½ cup sugar
*1 3-ounce package cream
  cheese, softened*
*1 1-pint box strawberries,
  hulled and thickly sliced*
*½ pint heavy (whipping)
  cream, lightly whipped*

Roll out the pastry to fit the bottom and sides of a 9-inch pie plate. Prick all over with a fork and bake in a 450° oven until browned, about 12 to 15 minutes. Let cool completely.

Bring the water to a boil in a small saucepan. Remove from the heat and stir in the gelatin, then the butter or margarine. In a small bowl, mix together the flour and sugar and stir the mixture into the saucepan. Heat, stirring, until the mixture comes to a boil. Transfer to a bowl and chill until thick and syrupy. (To speed this up, place the bowl in a larger bowl filled with ice cubes.)

Spread the cream cheese in a thin layer on the bottom of the pie shell. Arrange the strawberry slices on top. Pour the gelatin glaze over the berries and chill until set, about 2 hours.

Just before serving, garnish the pie with the whipped cream.
Yield: 6 to 8 servings.

Note: This pie is best served the day it is made.

Lemon Icebox Pie

❖

Of all the desserts served at Miss Mary's, the recipe for this refreshingly cool pie was the one most often requested. The pie has a graham cracker crust, a quickly assembled lemon filling, and golden meringue on top.

For the Crust

1½ cups crushed graham
   cracker crumbs
1 teaspoon sugar

½ stick (¼ cup) butter,
   melted

For the Filling and Meringue

3 eggs, separated
1 8-ounce can sweetened
   condensed milk (not
   evaporated milk)

½ cup freshly squeezed lemon
   juice
Grated rind from 1 lemon
6 tablespoons sugar

Stir together the graham cracker crumbs, 1 teaspoon sugar, and melted butter. Press into a 9-inch pie plate. Chill 10 minutes.

In a bowl, beat the egg yolks with the milk until well blended. Stir in the lemon juice and rind. Pour into the pie shell.

In another bowl, beat the egg whites until stiff. Gradually beat in the 6 tablespoons sugar. Spread the meringue over the filling.

Bake the pie in a 350° oven 15 minutes, or until a light golden brown. Chill well before serving.

Yield: 8 servings.

"In the Hollow"
Fresh Peach Cobbler

❖

No matter how much a guest had eaten for dinner, when Miss Mary's Fresh Peach Cobbler came to the table, there was always room for dessert. Served slightly warm from the oven, this golden-brown pastry is brimming with tender luscious peaches swimming in their juices.

For those unfamiliar with the term, a cobbler is an old-fashioned word for a deep-dish pie. The only real difference is that the fruit for a cobbler is cooked before it is turned into the pastry crust.

½ cup sugar
½ cup water
9 peaches, peeled and thickly
  sliced (about 7 cups slices)

Pinch salt
Recipe for 2-crust pastry
  (page 115)

In a large heavy saucepan, cook the sugar and water until the sugar dissolves. Add the peach slices and salt. Cover the pan and simmer the peaches until tender, about 5 minutes.

Divide the pastry into two portions, one about twice as large as the other. Roll out the larger ball to an 11-inch circle and fit into a deep-dish 9-inch pie pan. Roll out the other piece of pastry enough to cover the top of the pan.

Turn the peach slices and their cooking juices into the prepared pan. Cover with the top crust. Make a few slits in the crust for steam to escape, and pinch the edges together well.

Place the cobbler in a 450° oven (425° for a glass pan) and

bake for 10 minutes. Lower the oven to 350° (325° for the glass pan) and bake about 1 hour longer, or until the crust is golden brown.

Let cool slightly before serving. Serve with vanilla ice cream or whipped cream.

Yield: 9 servings.

Note: This recipe calls for peeled peach slices. The easiest way to peel peaches is to drop them, three at a time, into a large saucepan of boiling water. Leave the peaches in the water for about 30 seconds, and then remove with a slotted spoon; when cool enough to handle, the skins will slip right off.

January 29. A royal day, today has been. Quite early this morning our little band that remains at home started en route for the old home to see Pa and Ma or Grandpa and Grandma. A gladly greeting awaited us and a good dinner like Ma always cooks was ready even before the clock struck twelve. Dinner over, the boys indulged in some hearty jokes and then each one went to their farm work. Evening spent in Ma's room, and like a good mother she was studying about this thing or that that might be useful in my family. She gave me several things which will prove to be of much benefit, and which I appreciate.

Sue Dance Record's Diary, 1896.

Apricot Crescent Roll

❖

This delightfully delicious dessert is simple—a tender, flaky pastry dough is wrapped, jelly-roll style, around a thick puree of dried apricots and baked until delicately browned. Luscious fresh Lemon Sauce is served atop each slice. Although fairly easy to prepare, this is definitely a company dessert because dried apricots are rather an extravagance. When you taste this meltingly tender confection, though, you'll agree that it's worth making for any special occasion.

Crescent

1 16-ounce package dried
  apricots
⅓ cup sugar
1 cup water
Recipe for 2-crust pastry
  (page 115)

2 tablespoons butter or
  margarine
2 tablespoons sugar for top

Place the apricots, ⅓ cup sugar, and water in a saucepan. Bring to a boil. Reduce the heat, cover, and simmer until the apricots are tender, about 30 minutes. Let cool slightly and then puree. This is most easily done with a blender or food processor, but you may also use a food mill or even mash by hand with a fork. Place in the refrigerator, covered, for several hours or overnight.

Roll out the pastry to an 18 by 14-inch rectangle and spread with the apricot puree to within ½ inch of the edges. Beginning with a long edge, roll up jelly-roll style. Pinch the ends together, bend slightly to form a crescent shape, and transfer, seam side down, to a greased 9 by 13-inch baking pan. Dot with the butter and sprinkle with the 2 tablespoons sugar. Add water to depth of ¼ inch.

Bake the crescent in a 350° oven until golden brown, about 1½ hours. Serve at room temperature, sliced, with warm Lemon Sauce poured over each serving.

Yield: 8 to 10 servings.

Lemon Sauce

1 cup sugar
1 cup water
1 stick (½ cup) butter or
 margarine
6 tablespoons freshly squeezed
 lemon juice

2 tablespoons cornstarch,
 dissolved in 2 tablespoons
 water
1 cup heavy (whipping)
 cream, whipped until stiff

Place the sugar, water, butter or margarine, and lemon juice in a saucepan. Bring to a boil. Stir in the cornstarch mixture and cook a few moments longer, stirring constantly, until thickened. Serve warm over slices of Apricot Crescent Roll. Top with a dollop of freshly whipped cream.

Sweet Potato Pie

❖

Sweeter, lighter, and more brilliantly colored than pumpkin pie, this delicate custard pie is a hallmark of Southern cooking. If you've never sampled this, here's a chance to try it.

About 2 medium sweet potatoes
Recipe for 1-crust pastry (page 115)
½ stick (¼ cup) butter, softened
½ cup light or dark brown sugar

3 eggs
⅓ cup light corn syrup
⅓ cup milk
1 teaspoon vanilla extract
¼ teaspoon salt

Place the sweet potatoes in a saucepan and cover with water. Bring to a boil and continue boiling until the potatoes are tender, about 25 minutes. Drain. When cool enough to handle, peel off the skin and mash. You will need 1 cup of mashed potatoes.

Line a 9-inch pie plate with the pastry and prick all over with a fork. Bake in a 425° oven 10 minutes, or until very light brown.

In a medium bowl, cream the butter with the brown sugar. Beat in the eggs. Beat in the corn syrup, milk, vanilla, salt, and mashed sweet potatoes.

Turn the filling into the pie crust and bake in a 425° oven 10 minutes. Lower the heat to 325° and bake about 25 minutes longer, or until the filling is set and a knife inserted in the center comes out clean. Transfer to a rack to cool.

Yield: 8 servings.

Egg Pie

❖

This marvelously rich custard baked in a pie shell has the added benefit of being just about foolproof.

Recipe for 1-crust pastry   *2 tablespoons flour*
   (page 115)   *1 cup milk*
1 stick (½ cup) butter or   *2 eggs*
   margarine   *1 teaspoon vanilla extract*
½ cup sugar

Roll out the pastry to fit the bottom and sides of a 9-inch pie plate. Use a shallow pie pan for this recipe because the filling is not very deep. Bake the pastry in a 450° oven about 12 minutes, or until just beginning to brown. Remove from the oven and turn the temperature down to 350°.

In a medium saucepan, melt the butter or margarine. Remove from the heat and stir in the sugar and flour. Add the milk, eggs, and vanilla and beat well. Pour into the partially baked crust.

Place the pie in the 350° oven and bake 35 to 40 minutes, or until set and lightly browned along the edges. Let cool before serving. Refrigerate any leftovers.

Yield: 6 servings.

Variation: **Egg Meringue Pie.** Separate the eggs and use only the yolks in the filling. After the pie has baked, beat the egg whites until stiff and then gradually beat in ¼ cup sugar and ¼ teaspoon vanilla extract. Spread over the filling and return the pie to the oven for 15 minutes longer, or until the meringue is golden brown.

Bobo House Buttermilk Pie

❖

Fresh buttermilk pies are about as Southern as you can get, and anyone who's never sampled one has missed a real treat. The buttermilk gives an extra-fresh flavor and zippiness to the rich, creamy custard mixture.

Recipe for 1-crust pastry
  (page 115)
½ stick (¼ cup) butter or
  margarine
¾ cup sugar

2 tablespoons flour
Pinch salt
4 eggs, beaten lightly
1 tablespoon vanilla extract
⅔ cup buttermilk

Roll out the pastry and fit into a 9-inch pie plate. Bake the pastry in a 425° oven 12 minutes, or until it is lightly browned. Reduce the oven to 350°.

In a medium saucepan, melt the butter or margarine. Remove from the heat and stir in the sugar, flour, and salt. Add the eggs, vanilla, and buttermilk and mix well.

Pour the filling into the pie shell and bake the pie in the 350° oven about 45 minutes, or until set and lightly browned. The pie will puff up as it bakes and then sink as it cools. It is best served at room temperature or chilled.

Yield: 8 servings.

Note: Although in many recipes you may substitute a mixture of sweet milk and vinegar for buttermilk, for this pie you must use real cultured buttermilk, which is widely available in the dairy section of supermarkets.

Coconut Custard Pie

❖

One of the simplest of Miss Mary's recipes to fix, this was also one of the most popular. Originally, this rich pie was served only at Christmas, when fresh coconuts were available, but now that they can be purchased year-round, Coconut Custard Pie can be a welcome dessert in any season.

Recipe for 1-crust pastry
  (page 115)
1 cup milk
2 eggs, beaten slightly
1 tablespoon butter, melted
  in a medium saucepan

⅔ cup sugar
1 tablespoon flour
1 teaspoon vanilla extract
1 cup coarsely shredded
  coconut

Roll out the pastry and fit into a 9-inch pie plate. Prick all over with a fork and bake in a 400° oven 10 minutes, or until lightly browned.

Meanwhile, off heat, beat the milk and eggs into the melted butter in the saucepan. Stir together the sugar and flour and beat into the egg mixture. Stir in the vanilla and coconut.

Pour the filling into the crust and bake in the 400° oven 10 minutes. Reduce the heat to 350° and bake about 30 minutes longer, or until the filling is puffed and set and a knife inserted in the center comes out clean. Transfer the pie to a rack to cool. Serve at room temperature. Refrigerate any leftovers.

Yield: 8 servings.

Note: This pie is best made with fresh coconut (see page 196 for directions on cracking this hard-shelled nut), but you may substitute canned or packaged shredded coconut.

Chess Pie

❖

No book on Southern cooking would be complete without a recipe for Chess Pie, which has been described as tasting like pecan pie without the nuts. Dense, sweet, and buttery, this pie is also one of the easiest to prepare.

There are several theories as to how Chess Pie got its name. One is that in the days before refrigeration when pies were kept in pie chests, this pie, because of its high sugar content, was renowned for its keeping qualities—a real "chest" pie; with time, the *t* in chest was simply dropped. Yet another theory maintains that *chess* is a variation on *cheese*, and indeed, this pie is as rich as cheese pie. Finally, there's a story that someone asked a Southern cook what she was baking and she responded, "Jes' pie." Whatever the meaning of the name, this dessert is well worth adding to your repertoire.

Recipe for 1-crust pastry (page 115)
3 eggs
1½ cups sugar
1 teaspoon distilled white vinegar

1 teaspoon vanilla extract
1 tablespoon cornmeal, preferably white
1 stick (½ cup) butter, melted (do not substitute margarine)

Roll out the pastry to line a 9-inch pie plate. Fit into the plate and prick with a fork. Bake in a 425° oven 5 minutes, or until lightly browned.

Beat the eggs well. Stir in the sugar and beat again. Stir in the remaining ingredients and mix thoroughly. Pour into the pie shell.

Bake the pie in a 350° oven 45 minutes, or until puffed and golden brown. The pie will sink as it cools and acquire the texture of pecan pie filling. Serve at room temperature.

Yield: 8 servings.

March 19. The rain started my hopper running so I have spent the past few days making soap when I could leave the house. Really, nursing and making soap have been my special employments this week—I have a large barrel almost full and more to make. I know not of anything so useful about a home as good, old-fashioned lye soap. It is necessary to cleanliness, and I have had such good luck this time that I am very much rejoiced. Should I count the cost of wood, hopper, etc., not over 50¢ has been spent and not less than $150 has been made, should I buy the soap at the regular price of 5¢ per pound.

Sue Dance Record's Diary, 1896.

Oh-So-Good Pie

❖

Whoever named this pie when it emerged from Miss Mary's kitchen is no longer remembered, but the descriptive title is certainly apt. The pie is rather like a traditional Southern pecan pie, but without the cloying sweetness, and the filling can be made in no time.

Recipe for 1-crust pastry
  (page 115)
1 stick (½ cup) butter or
  margarine
1 cup sugar
2½ teaspoons distilled white
  vinegar
1 teaspoon cinnamon
½ teaspoon nutmeg

4 eggs
1 cup finely diced dates
½ cup coarsely chopped
  pecans
1 cup heavy (whipping)
  cream, whipped with
  2 tablespoons sugar until
  stiff

Roll out the dough to fit into a 9-inch pie plate (not a deep-dish plate). Prick the dough in several places with a fork and bake in a 450° oven about 12 minutes, or until just beginning to brown. Remove from the oven and lower the heat to 375° while preparing the filling.

In a medium saucepan, melt the butter or margarine. Remove from the heat and beat in the sugar, vinegar, cinnamon, and nutmeg. Add the eggs and beat until well mixed. Stir in the dates and pecans.

Pour the filling into the crust and bake until the pie is lightly browned and set, about 35 to 40 minutes. Serve slightly warm or at room temperature, with a dollop of whipped cream.

  Yield: 8 to 10 servings.

Classic Pecan Pie

❖

Here's the sublime Southern dessert that's become a favorite with all Americans. The filling is rich but not gummy and contains plenty of crunchy toasted pecans. It's a true indulgence that should be enjoyed any time you want a sinfully rich dessert.

Recipe for 1-crust pastry
  (page 115)
3 eggs, beaten
1 cup light corn syrup
1 cup sugar

1 teaspoon vanilla extract
3 tablespoons butter, melted
1 cup broken pecans
Whipped cream (optional)

Roll out the pastry to fit a 9-inch pie plate and arrange in the plate.

In a large bowl, stir together the eggs, corn syrup, sugar, vanilla, and melted butter very well. Stir in the pecans.

Pour the filling into the pie crust and stir lightly to distribute the pecans evenly.

Bake the pie in a 400° oven 10 minutes. Lower the heat to 350° and bake 1 hour longer. The filling will still be slightly moist and soft (but not runny), but will set fully as it cools. Serve with whipped cream, if desired.

Yield: 8 to 10 servings.

Chocolate Meringue Pie

❖

A rich puddinglike filling is topped by a light and delicate meringue. If you're looking for a stunning chocolate dessert that will impress guests, this is the one for you.

Recipe for 1-crust pastry
  (page 115)

Chocolate Filling

1½ *cups milk*
¾ *cup sugar*
¼ *cup flour*
¼ *cup unsweetened cocoa*

3 *egg yolks, at room*
   temperature
1 *teaspoon vanilla extract*
½ *stick (¼ cup) butter,*
   softened

Meringue

3 *egg whites, at room*
   temperature
⅛ *teaspoon salt*

½ *teaspoon vanilla extract*
6 *tablespoons sugar*

Roll out the pastry to line a 9-inch pie plate and fit the pastry into the plate. Prick all over with a fork and bake in a 425° oven for about 12 minutes, or until golden brown.

To make the filling, heat the milk to scalding in a saucepan or double boiler (you need not use a double boiler if you're careful, but if you want to take no chances on the egg yolks curdling, perhaps you should use one).

In a bowl, stir together the ¾ cup sugar, flour, and cocoa. Add about ½ cup of the hot milk to make a paste and then pour the mixture into the saucepan with the milk. Cook, stirring, until the mixture thickens and comes to a boil. Cook 2 minutes longer and remove from the heat.

Beat the egg yolks in a bowl. Gradually beat in several table-spoons of the hot mixture. Add the egg mixture to the saucepan and cook, stirring, over very low heat 2 minutes. Remove from the heat and add 1 teaspoon vanilla and the butter. Let cool, stirring occasionally, and then turn into the baked pie shell.

To make the meringue, beat the egg whites in a clean bowl with the salt and ½ teaspoon vanilla until stiff. Gradually beat in the 6 tablespoons sugar. When done, the mixture will be very stiff and glossy. Spread over the chocolate mixture, covering it completely.

Bake the pie in a 350° oven 15 minutes, or until the meringue is lightly browned. Let the pie cool to room temperature before serving. For best results, serve the pie the day it is made; if you refrigerate meringue, it often "weeps."

Yield: 8 servings.

January 14. Washday, and weather growing colder. Soap agent comes around. Of course agents always come when it is washday or some other day of hard work, but I never treat an agent badly. I would not want to be treated so myself should I want to act as an agent. A friend whom I had not seen for a long time comes and asks a favor which is cheerfully granted and besides tells me all about himself and family—his wife having lived with me for about a year. 'Tis nice to be remembered and loved by those who know you in everyday life at home and this girl always seemed to love me.

Sue Dance Record's Diary, 1896.

Fudge Pie

❖

This is one pie that explains the phrase "easy as pie," for it takes just a few ingredients, quickly mixed together, to make it. A rich, dense pie that tastes almost like an especially fudgy brownie, it is good served warm or at room temperature, with whipped cream or ice cream.

Recipe for 1-crust pastry
  (page 115)
2 eggs
1 cup sugar

1 stick (½ cup) butter, melted
¼ cup cocoa
¼ cup flour
1 teaspoon vanilla extract

Roll out the pastry and fit it into a 9-inch pie plate.

Beat the eggs in a medium bowl. Gradually beat in the sugar. When done, the mixture should be thick and pale yellow. Beat in the melted butter and cocoa. Add the flour and vanilla and beat just until incorporated.

Turn the chocolate mixture into the pie shell. Bake the pie in a 300° oven, or until set. Let cool on a rack. The pie will rise while baking and sink as it cools.

Yield: 6 to 8 servings.

Crustless Fudge Pie

❖

Not really a pie at all, this wonderfully rich dessert is more like an extra-chewy brownie that's been baked in a pie plate. Serve it in wedges. It's delicious warm from the oven, topped with a scoop of ice cream.

2 squares unsweetened chocolate
1 stick (½ cup) butter
2 eggs
¾ cup sugar
1 teaspoon vanilla extract
2 tablespoons flour
½ cup coarsely chopped pecans

In a small saucepan, over very low heat, melt the chocolate with the butter. Remove from heat.

Beat the eggs well in a medium bowl. Gradually beat in the sugar until the mixture is thick and pale. Beat in the melted chocolate mixture, then the vanilla and flour. Stir in the pecans.

Spread the batter evenly in a greased 9-inch pie plate (the batter will be only about 1 inch deep). Place the "pie" in a cold oven and turn the heat to 325°. Bake 30 minutes. Transfer to a rack to cool.

Yield: 8 servings.

Meringue-Topped Jam Pie

❖

You may use any flavor jam, but red jams, such as strawberry or seedless raspberry, will give the filling a lovely deep pink tint.

Recipe for 1-crust pastry
  (page 115)

Filling

4 egg yolks	*2 tablespoons flour*
1 cup sugar	*1 cup milk*
2 tablespoons butter, melted	*1 cup jam or preserves*

Topping

4 egg whites	*½ cup sugar*
⅛ teaspoon salt	*½ teaspoon vanilla extract*

Prepare the pastry and use it to line a deep 9-inch pie plate.

Beat the egg yolks in a medium bowl. Gradually beat in the 1 cup sugar. The mixture will be thick and pale yellow. Beat in the butter and flour, then the milk and jam.

Turn the mixture into the pie crust. Bake the custard in a 350° oven about 1 hour. The custard will be set but not firm. Let cool 15 minutes.

Meanwhile, make the meringue. In a clean bowl, beat the egg whites with the salt until nearly stiff. Gradually beat in the ½ cup sugar until the mixture is glossy. Beat in the vanilla. Spread over the filling.

Bake the pie 20 minutes longer, or until the meringue is a light golden brown. Let the pie cool on a rack to room temperature before serving.

Yield: 8 servings.

Caramel Meringue Pie

❖

Here's another rich meringue pie that you're unlikely to find outside the South. The filling is a luscious amber-colored caramel mixture that tastes somewhat like a divine butterscotch pudding.

Recipe for 1-crust pastry
  (page 115)

Caramel Filling

1¼ cups sugar, divided   ¼ cup flour
1½ cups milk   3 egg yolks
1 tablespoon butter   2 teaspoons vanilla extract

Meringue

3 egg whites, at room   ½ teaspoon vanilla extract
   temperature   6 tablespoons sugar
⅛ teaspoon salt

Roll out the pastry to line a 9-inch pie plate and fit the pastry into the plate. Prick all over with a fork and bake in a 425° oven for about 12 minutes, or until golden brown.

In a small heavy skillet or saucepan, cook ½ cup sugar until it forms a golden brown syrup. Do not let it burn or it will become bitter.

Meanwhile, in a saucepan or double boiler, heat the milk and butter to scalding (a double boiler will prevent the egg yolks from curdling, although if you're careful you can use a saucepan, too). Very carefully, add the caramel syrup to the milk. Heat until the syrup dissolves. Then remove from heat.

In a bowl, stir together the remaining ¾ cup sugar and flour.

Add about ½ cup of the hot milk mixture to make a paste and then pour the paste back into the saucepan. Cook, stirring, until the mixture thickens and comes to a boil. Cook 2 minutes longer and remove from the heat.

Beat the egg yolks in a bowl. Gradually beat in several table-spoons of the hot mixture. Add the egg mixture to the saucepan and cook, stirring, over very low heat 2 minutes. Remove from the heat and add the vanilla. Let cool, stirring occasionally, and then turn into the baked shell.

Follow the directions for mixing and baking the meringue in the recipe for Chocolate Meringue Pie (page 130).

Yield: 8 servings.

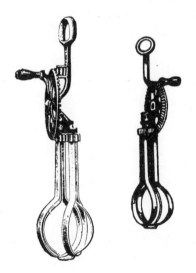

Glazed Prune Cake

❖

This rich, moist, old-fashioned spice cake is covered with a hot glaze as soon as it comes from the oven. The glaze permeates the cake, keeping it fresh and moist for days.

Cake Batter

1 cup dried prunes	2 cups flour
3 eggs	1 teaspoon baking soda
1½ cups sugar	1 teaspoon cinnamon
1 stick (½ cup) butter, melted	1 teaspoon nutmeg
1 cup buttermilk	1 teaspoon allspice
1 teaspoon vanilla extract	¼ teaspoon salt

Glaze

1 cup sugar	1 tablespoon white corn syrup
½ cup buttermilk	1 stick (½ cup) butter
½ teaspoon baking soda	1 teaspoon vanilla extract

Place the prunes in a saucepan and add enough water to cover completely. Bring to a boil. Then lower the heat and simmer 30 minutes. Drain and mash the prunes coarsely (remove pits if necessary).

In a large bowl, beat the eggs. Gradually beat in the sugar. When done, the mixture should be thick and pale. Beat in the melted butter, then the buttermilk and vanilla.

In another bowl, stir together the flour, baking soda, cinnamon, nutmeg, allspice, and salt. Beat into the liquid ingredients, just until incorporated. Beat in the prunes.

Turn the batter into a greased and floured 9 by 13-inch baking pan. Bake the cake in a 300° oven about 50 minutes, or until a toothpick inserted in the center comes out clean.

While the cake is baking, place all the ingredients for the glaze in a small saucepan. Bring to a boil, stirring. Cook until thick and frothy, about 2 minutes longer. As soon as the cake comes out of the oven, pour the glaze evenly over it. Let the cake cool on a rack.

Note: Because this cake is so moist, any leftovers should be stored in the refrigerator.

Yield: 20 servings.

February 7. Nothing special has happened today. Piecing quilts and making buttonholes has been the order of the day. Mrs. Williamson spent the evening with us and we had a fine time talking, sewing and eating hickory nuts.

Sue Dance Record's Diary, 1896.

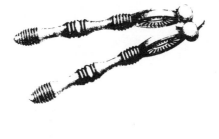

Sour Cream Cake

❖

This magnificently high cake has the dairy-fresh flavor of sour cream and a texture like that of an especially light pound cake. It's the kind of cake that's welcome in the summer with a bowl of fresh fruits.

6 eggs, separated
2 sticks (1 cup) butter,
  softened
2⅓ cups sugar
1 cup sour cream

1 teaspoon vanilla extract
3 cups flour
¼ teaspoon baking soda
¼ teaspoon salt

Beat the egg whites in a bowl until stiff. Set aside.

In a large bowl, cream the butter with the sugar. Beat in the egg yolks, then the sour cream and vanilla.

In another bowl, stir together the flour, baking soda, and salt. Beat into the creamed mixture just until moistened. Stir in one-third of the egg whites to lighten the batter and then fold in the rest gently but thoroughly.

Turn the batter into a greased and floured 9-inch tube pan. Bake the cake in a 300° oven 1¾ to 2 hours, or until a tooth-pick inserted in the center comes out clean. Let cool on a rack before removing from the pan.

Yield: 20 to 24 servings.

Dump Cake

❖

This cake got its name from the unusual—and amazingly simple
—technique of combining the ingredients, which are just
"dumped" into the baking pan. The cake departs from Miss
Mary's norm in that it calls for several convenience foods rather
than the fresh homemade ingredients she generally relied on. But
every once in a while, she or her cooks would hit on a novel
recipe like this one, and it quickly became a favorite because it
was just so easy to put together and so good to eat. This cake is
delicious served warm from the oven, with a scoop of vanilla
ice cream to enhance its fruity flavor.

*1 20-ounce can cherry pie
  filling
1 20-ounce can crushed
  pineapple, drained
1 cup shredded coconut*

*1 cup coarsely chopped pecans
1 box (2-layer size) golden or
  butter cake mix
1 stick (½ cup) butter, melted*

Spread the cherry pie filling in a greased 9 by 13-inch baking
pan. Arrange the pineapple over that and sprinkle with the
coconut and pecans.

In a mixing bowl, stir together the cake mix and melted butter
until crumbly. Sprinkle evenly over the mixture in the pan. Pat
down lightly.

Bake the cake in a 350° oven 1¾ hours, or until it is golden
brown on top.

Yield: 15 servings.

Mississippi Mud Cake

❖

This deep, dark chocolate cake contains lots of goodies just waiting to be discovered. Similar in texture to a cakelike brownie, it is filled with plenty of pecans and covered with a layer of melted marshmallows topped by a rich chocolate icing.

Cake

2 sticks (1 cup) butter,
  softened
2 cups sugar
4 eggs
1 teaspoon vanilla extract
1⅔ cups flour

⅔ cup unsweetened cocoa,
  sifted if lumpy
2 teaspoons baking powder
2 cups coarsely chopped
  pecans
1 10-ounce bag marshmallows

Icing

½ stick (¼ cup) butter,
  softened
¼ cup cocoa, sifted if lumpy
1 teaspoon vanilla extract

⅛ teaspoon salt
1½ cups sifted confectioners'
  sugar
2 tablespoons milk

First make the cake. In a large bowl, cream the butter with the sugar. Beat in the eggs, then the vanilla.

In another bowl, stir together the flour, cocoa, and baking powder. Beat into the creamed ingredients and stir in the pecans.

Turn the batter into a well-greased 9 by 13-inch baking pan. Bake in a 350° oven 35 minutes, or until the cake barely tests done with a toothpick. (The toothpick will be moist, with a few bits of batter sticking to it; it will not be *coated* with batter). Spread the marshmallows on top in an even layer and bake 5 to

10 minutes longer, or until the marshmallows are a very pale golden brown. Let the cake cool thoroughly. Do not remove from pan.

In a small bowl, cream together all ingredients for the icing. If the icing is too thick, thin with a bit more milk; if too thin, beat in a bit more sugar. After the cake has cooled, spread the icing in a thin layer over the marshmallows. Let icing set at least 10 minutes before cutting the cake.

Yield: 20 servings.

January 16. I attended the burial of little Leta S. (daughter of Wm. and Mattie S.) this evening. She was about six years old. She died from pneumonia; having had whooping cough all winter, she lived only a short time after pneumonia set up. Mr. Jimmie S. died today. I feel sorry for his bereaved companion and loved ones. Mr. Jim was a nice, good boy and a friend of my husband and myself in his younger days. In thinking of him, I recall many pleasant occasions in bygone days.

Sue Dance Record's Diary, 1896.

Chocolate Syrup Cake

❖

This recipe is Louise Crutcher's (she's Mary Bobo's daughter). When I visited Louise, her brother, Charles, asked if I had yet sampled his sister's Chocolate Syrup Cake and I replied that it was the next cake recipe I was testing. Recalling that in my cake cookbook I had suggested that none of the cakes required any icing, Charles made a point of stressing that I had sure better put some chocolate icing on Louise's cake. That I did, and the result was delicious—rich and dark and chocolatey, a real must for chocoholics.

Cake

1 stick (½ cup) butter, softened
⅔ cup sugar
4 eggs

2 cups chocolate syrup
2 cups flour
1 teaspoon baking powder

Icing

2 ounces unsweetened chocolate
3 tablespoons butter
1 teaspoon vanilla extract

About ¼ cup milk
About 2 cups sifted confectioners' sugar

First make the cake. In a large bowl, cream the butter with the sugar. Beat in the eggs very well, then the chocolate syrup.

In another bowl, stir together the flour and baking powder. Beat into the chocolate mixture just until moistened.

Turn the batter into a greased and floured 9 by 13-inch baking pan, spreading it evenly. Bake the cake in a 350° oven 35 to 40 minutes, or until a toothpick inserted in the center comes out clean. Transfer to a rack to cool.

When the cake has cooled completely, make the icing. Melt the chocolate and butter in a saucepan. Transfer to a mixing bowl and beat in the vanilla and half the milk. Beat in the confectioners' sugar and enough additional milk to make an icing of good spreading consistency. Spread over the cake and let the icing set at least 10 minutes before cutting the cake. Serve directly from the pan, cut into squares.

Yield: 20 servings.

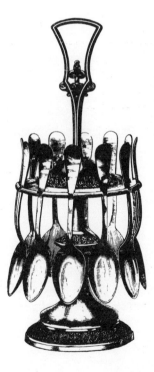

Glazed Apricot Cake

❖

This is a lovely, fine-textured cake that's something of a cross between a pound cake and a light sponge cake. Apricot nectar goes into the batter and also forms a glaze on the finished cake.

4 eggs, separated
2 sticks (1 cup) butter,
  softened
2⅓ cups sugar, divided
1⅓ cups apricot nectar,
  divided

Grated rind of 1 lemon
1½ teaspoons vanilla extract
2½ cups plus 1 tablespoon
  flour
2½ teaspoons baking powder
¼ teaspoon salt

Beat the egg whites until stiff. Set aside.

In a large bowl, cream the butter with 2 cups sugar. Beat in the egg yolks. Then beat in 1 cup apricot nectar, the lemon rind, and vanilla.

In another bowl, stir together the flour, baking powder, and salt. Beat into the creamed mixture, then fold in the egg whites gently but thoroughly.

Turn the batter into a greased and floured angel food or tube cake pan. Bake the cake in a 350° oven 1 to 1¼ hours, or until a toothpick inserted into the center of the cake comes out clean.

Just before the cake finishes baking, heat the remaining ⅓ cup sugar with the remaining ⅓ cup apricot nectar just until the mixture starts to boil (stir to dissolve the sugar). When the cake is done, transfer the pan to a rack and slowly pour the hot apricot syrup over the top. Let the cake remain in the pan until cool.

Yield: 16 to 20 servings.

Lemon Pound Cake

❖

This is a densely textured, butter-flavored pound cake that's perfect whenever you want a simple dessert. The fresh lemon peel in the batter gives it a lively and slightly exotic taste.

2 sticks (1 cup) butter, softened	1 teaspoon vanilla extract
2 cups sugar	1 cup milk
5 eggs	3½ cups flour
Grated rind of 1 lemon	½ teaspoon baking powder

In a large bowl, cream the butter with the sugar. Beat in the eggs, then the lemon rind, vanilla, and milk.

In another bowl, stir together the flour and baking powder. Beat into the creamed mixture just until thoroughly incorporated.

Turn the batter into a greased and floured 9-inch tube pan. Bake the cake in a 350° oven 1¼ hours, or until a toothpick inserted in the center comes out clean. Transfer to a rack to cool. Let cool completely before slicing.

Yield: 16 to 20 servings.

Burnt-Sugar Cake with Caramel Icing

❖

This cake has a fine subtle flavor from the "burnt" sugar, which, of course, isn't really burnt but simply cooked to a rich golden brown. The fudgelike caramel icing makes an ideal complement to the cake.

Cake

1½ cups sugar, divided
¾ cup water
1½ sticks (¾ cup) butter, softened

2 eggs
1 teaspoon vanilla extract
2½ cups flour
1½ teaspoons baking powder

Caramel Icing

1 cup light or dark brown sugar

5½ tablespoons butter, divided
¼ cup milk

Place ½ cup sugar in a heavy saucepan. Cook, stirring, over medium heat until it melts and turns a light brown color. Be careful not to let it get too brown, or it will indeed taste burnt. Gradually stir in the water until the sugar dissolves (the sugar may form a lump when the water is added; if this happens, cook over low heat until the sugar dissolves). Let cool.

In a large bowl, cream the 1½ sticks butter with the remaining 1 cup sugar. Beat in the eggs, then the vanilla and burnt-sugar syrup.

In another bowl, stir together the flour and baking powder. Beat into the creamed mixture just until moistened.

Turn the batter into a greased and floured 9 by 13-inch baking pan. Bake the cake in a 350° oven 40 minutes, or until a toothpick inserted in the center comes out clean. Transfer to a rack to cool before icing.

To make the icing, combine the brown sugar, 4 tablespoons butter, and milk in a saucepan. Cook until the butter melts and the sugar dissolves. Then continue cooking, without stirring, until the mixture reaches 238° to 240° on a candy thermometer. Remove from the heat and add the remaining butter. Let sit until the butter melts. Then beat with a heavy spoon until the icing is of good spreading consistency.

Ice the cake in the baking pan. Pour the caramel icing over the cake and spread it as quickly as possible. If it is handled very little, the icing will have a lovely sheen; if spread too much, though, it will become dull and granular. Let icing set at least 10 minutes before cutting the cake.

Yield: 20 servings.

Coconut-Topped Oatmeal Cake

❖

This deliciously moist cake has the flavor of a spicy coconut-oatmeal cookie, and the baked-on glaze is easy to prepare and invitingly attractive.

Cake

1¼ cups boiling water
1 cup quick-cooking oats
1 stick (½ cup) butter,
    softened
⅔ cup granulated sugar
⅔ cup light or dark brown
    sugar

2 eggs
1 teaspoon vanilla extract
1⅓ cups flour
1 teaspoon baking soda
¼ teaspoon salt

Glaze

½ stick (¼ cup) butter
⅔ cup light or dark brown
    sugar

½ cup light cream (or half
    and half)
1 cup shredded coconut

Pour the boiling water over the oats in a bowl and let stand while preparing the rest of the batter.

In a large bowl, cream the butter with the sugars. Beat in the eggs, then the vanilla.

In another bowl, stir together the flour, baking soda, and salt. Beat into the creamed ingredients, along with the oats.

Spread the batter evenly in a greased and floured 9 by 13-inch baking pan. Bake the cake in a 350° oven 30 minutes, or until a toothpick inserted in the center comes out clean.

Meanwhile, combine the glaze ingredients in a saucepan.

Cook, stirring, until the butter melts and the mixture just begins to boil. Spread over the baked cake and return to the oven for 10 minutes.

Yield: 16 servings.

Note: This cake is best served directly from the baking pan, because if it's tipped out, the glaze will come off.

January 31. Sion and Dance started early this morning to Tullahoma for their Pa. He returned about 4 o'clock and received a hearty welcome. We were glad to see him and then what a big treat of nice bananas he brought. The children always expect a nice treat when Pa comes home from a trip, and I am always one of the children when "goodies" are in order.

Sue Dance Record's Diary, 1896.

Coca-Cola–Marshmallow Cake

❖

The ingredients in this cake may seem a bit odd, but the result is delectable. The marshmallows melt when baked into tiny pockets of sweet tastiness, and the Coke lends a pleasant, almost spicy flavor. A creamy walnut icing tops off this popular dessert.

Cake

2 eggs
1½ cups sugar
½ cup vegetable oil
½ cup buttermilk (or use "soured" milk: place 1½ teaspoons distilled white vinegar in a measuring cup and fill to the ½-cup mark with milk; stir)

1 teaspoon vanilla extract
2½ cups flour
½ teaspoon baking soda
1 cup Coca-Cola, measured without foam
1½ cups miniature marshmallows

Icing

½ stick (¼ cup) butter
1½ tablespoons Coca-Cola
2 cups confectioners' sugar

½ teaspoon vanilla extract
½ cup coarsely chopped walnuts

First make the cake. Beat the eggs in a large bowl. Gradually beat in the sugar. When done, the mixture should be thick and pale yellow. Beat in the oil, buttermilk, and vanilla.

In another bowl, stir together the flour and baking soda. Beat this into the liquid ingredients alternately with the cola. Stir in the marshmallows.

Turn the batter into a greased and floured 9 by 13-inch baking pan. Bake the cake in a 350° oven 35 to 40 minutes, or until a toothpick inserted in the center comes out clean. Transfer to a rack to cool.

When the cake is completely cool, make the icing: Heat the butter and cola in a saucepan until the butter has melted. Remove from the heat and stir in the sugar and vanilla. Beat well. If too stiff, thin with a few drops of cola. Stir in the nuts. Spread the icing over the cake in the pan. Let icing set at least 10 minutes before cutting the cake.

Yield: about 16 servings.

Billy Goat Cookies

❖

The origin of this cookie's unusual name has been lost, but perhaps it derives from the fact that billy goats are known for their propensity to eat anything—and these plump drop cookies are filled with just about everything: dates, nuts, and spices.

⅓ cup (5⅓ tablespoons)
* butter, softened*
⅔ cup sugar
1 egg
1 tablespoon milk
½ teaspoon vanilla extract
1⅓ cups flour
¼ teaspoon baking soda

1 teaspoon baking powder
½ teaspoon cinnamon
¼ teaspoon ground cloves
8 ounces chopped dates
* (about 1½ cups)*
⅔ cup chopped walnuts or
* pecans*

In a large bowl, cream the butter with the sugar. Beat in the egg, milk, and vanilla.

In a medium bowl, stir together the flour, baking soda, baking powder, cinnamon, and cloves. Beat into the creamed mixture and then stir in the dates and nuts.

Drop the batter by heaping teaspoonfuls onto greased baking sheets. Bake the cookies in a 375° oven about 20 minutes, or until lightly browned. Transfer to racks to cool.

Yield: about 3 dozen cookies.

Spiced Molasses Cookies

❖

These cookies are soft and chewy, with a subtle, spicy flavor and a dark molasses color.

1½ sticks (¾ cup) butter, softened	2½ cups flour
1 cup light or dark brown sugar	1 teaspoon baking soda
	¼ teaspoon salt
2 eggs	1 teaspoon cinnamon
¼ cup molasses	1 teaspoon ground ginger
	½ teaspoon ground cloves

In a large bowl, cream the butter with the brown sugar. Beat in the eggs, then the molasses.

In another bowl, stir together the flour, baking soda, salt, and spices. Beat into the creamed mixture.

Drop the cookies by heaping teaspoonfuls onto greased baking sheets. Bake the cookies in a 350° oven about 10 minutes, or until they are lightly browned (they will still be somewhat soft, but if you insert a toothpick into the center, it will come out clean). Transfer the cookies to a rack to cool.

Yield: about 3 dozen cookies.

Old-Fashioned Strawberry Shortcake

❖

Here's the traditional recipe for fresh strawberry shortcake, complete with homemade shortcakes (fresh, buttery biscuits). It's a perfect dessert for springtime entertaining because all the preparation can be done in advance. You can even let your guests assemble their own desserts.

Shortcakes

2 cups flour	*¼ teaspoon salt*
1 tablespoon granulated sugar	*½ stick (¼ cup) butter*
2 teaspoons baking powder	*¾ cup milk*

Filling

1 quart fresh strawberries, hulled and thickly sliced	*2 tablespoons confectioners' sugar*
⅓ cup granulated sugar	*Butter*
½ pint heavy (whipping) cream	

Prepare the shortcakes. In a large bowl, stir together the flour, sugar, baking powder, and salt. With a pastry cutter or two knives, cut in the butter until the mixture resembles coarse meal. Stir in the milk.

Turn the mixture out onto a lightly floured board and knead for just about 30 seconds. Form into a ball and roll out ½-inch thick. Cut into rounds with a floured 2-inch cutter and place on a greased baking sheet.

Bake the biscuits in a 450° oven 20 minutes, or until light golden brown. Transfer to a rack to cool.

Toss the strawberries with the granulated sugar. Let sit in the refrigerator at least 1 hour before serving.

Whip the cream with the confectioners' sugar until stiff.

To serve, split the biscuits and butter the cut surfaces lightly (this keeps the biscuits moist and adds to their richness). Put 2 biscuits into each of 6 serving bowls, spooning strawberries between the layers and on top. Top with whipped cream.

Yield: 12 shortcakes (6 servings).

February 27. Patch, patch, patch, will there ever be an end to patching? Yet there is no happier time to me than when I know that every child's clothes are patched and ready for wear. Today has also been used in preparing our Quarterly Meeting tomorrow. Eula and I have baked a nice cake, Mary has dressed a fat hen and other preparations in the way of house cleaning and cooking have been going on in general.

Sue Dance Record's Diary, 1896.

Banana Custard Pudding

❖

In Miss Mary's kitchen, this homey dessert reached the sublime, with its rich vanilla custard and fluff of golden brown meringue.

¾ cup sugar, divided　　　　*3 eggs, separated*
3 tablespoons flour　　　　*1 teaspoon vanilla extract*
⅛ teaspoon salt　　　　*1 11-ounce box vanilla wafers*
2 cups milk　　　　*6 very ripe bananas*
1 tablespoon butter

In a heavy saucepan, stir together ½ cup sugar, the flour, and salt. Add enough milk to make a paste and then stir in the remaining milk. Cook the mixture over moderate heat, stirring, until it thickens and comes to a boil. Add the butter and cook over very low heat 5 minutes, stirring occasionally.

In a small bowl, beat the egg yolks. Gradually, beat in about ½ cup of the hot mixture. Pour the yolks into the saucepan and cook, stirring, over very low heat 1 minute. Remove from the heat and stir in the vanilla.

Arrange one third of the vanilla wafers in a 2-quart casserole. Slice 2 bananas over these and cover with one-third of the custard. Repeat layers twice more.

In a bowl, beat the egg whites until stiff. Beat in the remaining ¼ cup sugar. Continue beating until very glossy. Spread this meringue over the pudding.

Bake the pudding in a 425° oven about 5 minutes, or until the peaks of the meringue are golden brown. Serve at room temperature or chilled.

Yield: 8 servings.

Tennessee Bar-B-Que

A TENNESSEE BAR-B-QUE is very different from what most of the rest of the country means when they say, "Come on over for a barbecue!" Although in most areas a barbecue means hot dogs, burgers, chicken, or steaks cooked outdoors on a grill, in Lynchburg this type of meal is simply called a "grill-out." Bar-b-que is pronounced just as it's spelled in this state, with an emphasis on that second "B."

As one man explained it, "Bar-b-que is the whole kit and kaboodle here." And this always means pork—a whole joint (front quarter) or ham (hind quarter)—cooked slowly in a pit over hickory-wood coals. It used to be that everyone had a bar-b-que pit dug in the backyard, but nowadays most people build their pits out of rock so they're up off the ground and don't require constant backbreaking bending to tend to the meat.

A Tennessee bar-b-que is usually prepared for anywhere from 150 to 200 people, or even more. Not so many years ago, candidates running for office would throw a bar-b-que for the entire town. There's *always* a bar-b-que on the Fourth of July, and bar-b-ques occur often throughout the rest of the summer. As someone told me, "Well, it's like this: You get two or three people standing around and one of them will say, 'Heck, let's have a bar-b-que.' So they'll kill their own pig and invite their friends. Of course, there's always someone there with a fiddle, so there'll be a square dance, too. And people will play ball and pitch horseshoes."

Making a proper bar-b-que is no easy job, and the people who excel at it take a lot of pride in their skill. Timing is the most critical part of making good barbecued pork. The meat should cook slowly for a full twenty-four hours, and that means staying up all night to tend to the coals. As one expert said, "There's a real art to it, and you don't want anyone else messing with your work. There's a time to turn the meat over, and a time not to. And there's a time to put sauce on it, and a time not to. You want to have it done but not too quickly, or it'll be dry and burned."

Speaking of sauce, Tennessee bar-b-que sauce isn't like the bottled ones available in supermarkets. Bar-b-que dip, as it's called, is a lot thinner, and every cook has his own closely guarded secret recipe. The sauce is put on the meat when it has nearly finished cooking, and then when guests eat the pork, they dip their pieces into any sauce that remains.

While a bar-b-que always means roast pork, a lot of other foods can be served as well. Goat is very common; the shoulders and hams are roasted over hot coals, while the rest of the animal, along with plenty of dried hot peppers, goes into a soup that's also dished up. Sometimes bar-b-ques are held in conjunction with coon or fox hunts; any fox that's caught wouldn't be eaten, but the coon very well might be.

Old-time bar-b-ques were never combined with fish fries, but today people often enjoy both together. Freshly caught catfish are deep-fried in a big iron pot, and after about a dozen fish have been cooked, some of the fish-flavored oil is tipped out into another pot for frying hush puppies, the cornmeal cakes that are the traditional accompaniment.

Fish fries are also often held on their own. This happens when several men go off camping down by the river. After they've been gone for a couple of days, family and friends will join them for a fish fry. Usually word gets around that something's up, and as many as fifty or sixty people have been known to come by for dinner.

Miss Mary's cousin, Frank Bobo, the head distiller at Jack Daniel's, has been cooking up bar-b-ques for about twenty-five or thirty years now. As he describes it:

Traditionally on the Fourth of July, most folks in rural Tennessee are either preparing a bar-b-que for a crowd or planning to attend one at a neighbor's house. Since a bar-b-que (country style) requires a whole lot of know-how, a lot of tender loving care, and several hours of preparation, it is usually prepared for no less than twenty-five people and sometimes hundreds.

The menu consists of pork bar-b-que, catfish and hush puppies, and all the trimmings, which consists of potato salad, slaw, pickles (both sweet and dill), sliced raw onions, charcoaled onions, fresh tomatoes (quartered), a favorite beverage such as lemonade, and a favorite dessert or watermelon. Other foods often served at a bar-b-que are deviled eggs and baked beans.

Bar-B-Que Pork

❖

The pork shoulders are cooked over an open pit constructed so that the meat cooks 18 to 20 inches above the hickory coals. The hot coals are made in a separate fireplace and transferred to the pit with a shovel. Hickory wood is a necessity since the coals seem to be hotter and last much longer than other woods. Also, the hickory flavor is most pleasing.

Sauce

2 fresh pork shoulders, 12 to 13 pounds each
Salt
3 cups vegetable oil, plus additional oil for basting
2 cups distilled white vinegar, plus additional vinegar for basting
6 lemons, halved
1 bottle steak sauce, such as 57 Sauce
1 bottle Worcestershire sauce
2 onions, minced
1 cup light or dark brown sugar
1 teaspoon salt
1 teaspoon hot pepper sauce
Red pepper, to taste
Black pepper, to taste

Prepare the meat for the pit by rubbing it with salt. After you have a smooth bed of hot coals under the grill and the temperature directly underneath the grill is such that you can leave your hand for 3 seconds before you have to move it, the meat is ready to place on the grill. Start the meat with the skin side down and cook slowly for about a couple of hours. As it cooks, baste it with a mixture of vegetable oil and vinegar in equal proportions. This helps prevent the meat from blackening in case the fire gets a little too hot. After 2 hours, turn the meat over and cook for another 2 hours, keeping fresh hot coals in the pit all the time. Turn the meat over again and cover loosely with cardboard or something that would not be detrimental to the flavor.

Meanwhile, make the Bar-B-Que Sauce: Place the 3 cups oil, 2 cups vinegar and all remaining ingredients in a saucepan. Bring to a boil. Then lower the heat and let simmer 1 hour, stirring occasionally.

After 6 hours of cooking the meat, it's time to baste the meat with the sauce. The sauce should be mopped on the meat every time it is turned, which should be done as often as needed to prevent the meat from burning or charring too badly. Cooking time will vary, depending on the thickness of the meat and the fire. A good 12 hours are usually needed to cook the bar-b-que. A test for doneness is to twist the hock of the joint with your hand. If it twists easily, then it is done. To serve the meat, it should be pulled or torn from the bone by hand, rather than carved with a knife.

Yield: 25 servings.

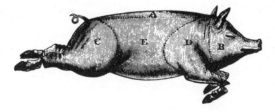

Hush Puppies

❖

After the fish are fried, it is time to cook the Hush Puppies. They are cooked in the same oil used to cook the fish. This gives the puppies flavor.

The name comes from back when folks, after cooking fish over a campfire, mixed together some extra cornmeal and water, fried it, and gave it to the howling dogs to keep them quiet.

4 cups cornmeal, preferably white
6 onions, minced
2 green peppers, minced
¼ cup flour
½ cup light or dark brown sugar
2 teaspoons salt
1 teaspoon sage

Black pepper, to taste, about 1 teaspoon (you should be able to see flecks of it)
4 eggs, beaten lightly
About 1 cup buttermilk (enough to make the mixture wet but not so thin as to be runny)
Corn oil for frying

Mix together the cornmeal, onions, peppers, flour, brown sugar, salt, sage, and pepper. Beat together the eggs and buttermilk and stir in. Add more buttermilk, if necessary.

Heat the oil to about 350°. Using two teaspoons, one in each hand, dip into the batter with one and scoop out a rounded spoonful, then push the batter out of the spoon into the oil with the other spoon. When the mixture hits the hot oil, it will form a ball and float. If the consistency is perfect, the balls will flip themselves over when one side browns. When brown on both sides, remove with a slotted spoon and drain on paper towels. Serve hot.

Yield: 25 servings.

Note: For a hush-puppy recipe to serve 6, use the proportions below:

1 cup cornmeal, preferably white
1 onion, minced
½ green pepper, minced
1 tablespoon flour
2 tablespoons brown sugar

½ teaspoon salt
¼ teaspoon sage
About ¼ teaspoon black pepper
1 egg
¼ to ⅓ cup buttermilk

Charcoaled Onions

❖

Charcoaled onions are very good and always go over big with the crowd. Allow at least one onion per person. Place the onion on a square of foil. Place a large pat of butter on top, along with salt and black pepper. Bring the sides of the foil up and twist at the top. Place on top of grill and cook for approximately 30 minutes, or until soft. Serve hot in the foil.

April 17. Well, Mr. R. knew how much we all loved fish, and knowing that we had a few the boys had caught, he brought more large fish. And, oh, what a delightful supper we had tonight. I never enjoyed a meal better. Really, fish is quite a rarity, now, with us. We have been trying our best to buy from hackman, but he could not get them, and we have been compelled to do without any. Oh, how tired I am tonight. I have been working hard all day, finishing my soap. I have made about 55 gallons and am so delighted with my luck. But I had good grease and lye. Mr. R. told me when I began to test the lye that he, like the old woman, could tell when lye was strong enough. He said to put an egg in it and if it was strong enough, the egg would sink or swim. He had forgotten which. Poor world, without ole women.

Sue Dance Record's Diary, 1896.

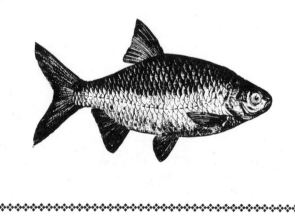

Catfish

❖

Once the Bar-B-Que Pork is just about cooked, it's time to think about the catfish. They are always cooked out of doors just before serving time so they will be hot. They should be cooked in deep fat, preferably corn oil. The traditional way of cooking catfish in Tennessee is in an old wash kettle swung over an open wood fire. The catfish are washed, salted, and mealed in cornmeal just before cooking.

A good-size fish to cook this way is one that weighs ¾ pound to 1 pound.

Salt
1 whole catfish per serving,
  cleaned, gutted, and with
  the head cut off

Cornmeal, preferably white
Corn oil for deep frying

Salt the fish and coat it well with the meal.

Heat the oil to 375°. Add the fish to the pot, but do not overcrowd. Catfish require a little more time than scaly fish, so after they float you should leave them cooking in the oil for another minute or so. Cooking time is approximately 10 minutes for each batch, providing the oil ranges from 350° to 375°.

When the fish are cooked, drain on paper towels and serve immediately.

Slaw

❖

This slaw may be prepared in advance since it will keep several days. It goes well with the pork and fish.

Slaw

9 pounds cabbage, shredded   6 green peppers, chopped
6 large onions, chopped   6 cups sugar

Dressing

3 cups vegetable oil   1 tablespoon salt
3 cups distilled white vinegar   1 tablespoon celery seed
1 tablespoon dry mustard

In a large bowl, mix together the cabbage, onions, peppers, and sugar.

In a medium saucepan, mix together all ingredients for the dressing and bring to a boil. While hot, pour over the cabbage mixture and stir well. Chill several hours before serving.

Yield: 25 servings.

Note: For Miss Mary's Cabbage Slaw, serving 8 to 10, see page 87.

Potato Salad

❖

A bar-b-que wouldn't be complete without some good potato salad. This potato salad may be prepared the day before and refrigerated.

20 *medium potatoes, unpeeled*
2 *cups mayonnaise, or to taste*
1 *8-ounce can pimientos,*
   diced
6 *hard-cooked eggs, chopped*
2 *cups chopped celery*

1 *pound Cheddar cheese,*
   finely diced
2 *cups chopped sweet pickles*
1 *cup chopped green olives*
Salt, to taste
Paprika, to garnish

Boil the potatoes until they pierce easily with a fork. Drain and let cool a while. Remove the skins and dice the potatoes.

Stir in all remaining ingredients, except the paprika. Mix carefully but avoid mashing. Before serving, sprinkle with paprika.
Yield: 25 servings.

Note: For Miss Mary's Country Potato Salad, serving 4, see page 89.

Deviled Eggs

❖

Here's another item always served at a Lynchburg bar-b-que.

2 dozen hard-cooked eggs,
  shelled and halved
  lengthwise
1 cup mayonnaise, or to taste
4 teaspoons prepared mustard

½ cup finely chopped sweet
  pickles
1 teaspoon salt
½ teaspoon pepper
Sliced pimiento-stuffed olives,
  as garnish

Scoop the yolks from the whites. Set the whites aside. Mash the yolks with a fork and stir in the mayonnaise, mustard, pickles, salt, and pepper.

With a spoon, carefully stuff the filling into the egg whites. Garnish with the olive slices. Chill until ready to serve.

Yield: 48 deviled eggs.

Baked Beans

❖

This dish is baked indoors and brought out just before serving the bar-b-que.

4 cans (about 28 ounces each) pork and beans
1 cup finely chopped onion
2 cups finely chopped green pepper
¾ cup catsup
½ cup molasses
½ teaspoon Worcestershire sauce
⅓ teaspoon pepper
20 slices bacon

Mix together all ingredients except the bacon and turn into a large greased casserole. Top with the bacon slices.

Bake the casserole, uncovered, in a 375° oven 1½ hours.

Yield: 25 servings.

Note: To make Baked Beans for 6 people, use the following proportions and bake only 1 hour.

1 can (about 28 ounces) pork and beans
¼ cup chopped onion
½ cup chopped green pepper
3 tablespoons catsup
2 tablespoons molasses
Dash Worcestershire sauce
⅛ teaspoon pepper
5 slices bacon

Cucumber Pickles. Apple worms have contributed to the flavor of all the natural cider and vinegar in the history of man. My own vinegar, home-made, of wormy windfall fruit, transforms my cucumbers into pickles as good as, or a shade better than the dill pickles of New York delicatessens. This makes them ultimate to me. I take a 10-by-3-inch pickle, twelve to twenty-four hours old, out of the jar from under the grape leaf and eat one entire every meal. My vinegar is so good I am not sure it is vinegar, and I don't know whether to drink it or make pickles in it. When I pick up every wormy apple or peach under the tree to make the vinegar in which to pickle the cucumbers, I *think* that I am working against next year's generation of fruit worms, although if I ever recover what my grandfathers knew, my apples will not have worms. Theirs didn't, nor did I ever hear them mention that insects bothered their cucumbers.

On Man and the Good Life. Leaves from the Notebook of Emmett Gowen.

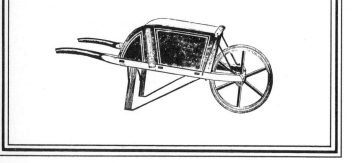

Black-Eyed Peas

❖

Although this recipe requires three days to prepare, there's really very little actual work involved. What makes it special is soaking the peas in the liquid in which the ham hocks cooked. The resulting dish has a marvelous smoked flavor, and is delicious served plain or with Texas Hot relish (page 174).

1 pound smoked ham hocks or shank	*1 large onion, diced*
	1 green pepper, diced
¼ pound smoked hog jowl (if available)	*1 teaspoon dry mustard*
	½ teaspoon salt
2 quarts water	*½ teaspoon pepper*
1 pound dried black-eyed peas	

On the first day, place the ham hocks and hog jowl (if used) in a large heavy saucepan with the water. Bring to a boil. Reduce the heat and simmer, covered, 2 hours. Remove the ham hocks and jowl and when cool enough to handle, dice the meat, discarding the skin and bones. Chill overnight in the liquid.

On the second day, remove the hardened fat from the liquid. Wash the peas and remove any that look spoiled. Add to the pot and chill overnight.

On the third day, add the onion, green pepper, mustard, salt, and pepper. Bring to a boil. Simmer, uncovered, stirring occasionally, about 2 hours, or until the peas are tender and most of the liquid has evaporated.

Yield: 8 to 10 servings.

Texas Hot

❖

This spicy, fresh relish is served on top of peas or beans—either Black-Eyed Peas (previous recipe), green beans, crowder peas, or just about any other type of bean. The relish is hot, so a little goes far. For best results, let the flavors mingle in the refrigerator for at least an hour before serving (overnight is even better).

1 tomato, chopped
1 small onion, minced
1 green pepper, minced
1 pod hot red or green
  pepper, seeded and finely
  minced (or substitute ½
  teaspoon hot pepper sauce)

1½ tablespoons distilled
  white vinegar
⅓ cup water
1 tablespoon sugar
¼ teaspoon salt
⅛ teaspoon pepper

Mix together all ingredients well. Cover and chill until ready to serve with beans. Any leftover sauce may be kept in the refrigerator for up to 1 week.

Yield: about 2½ cups, or 8 to 10 servings.

Holiday Foods

As IS TRUE just about everywhere else in this country, the Christmas season in Lynchburg is celebrated with plenty of festivities and good cheer. There are even more of the neighborly visits that people in this rural part of Tennessee enjoy so much throughout the rest of the year. Thus, while Christmas Eve and dinner on Christmas Day are reserved for kinfolk, on New Year's at least one friend always holds a big party. And on just about every other day during the holiday season, there's an informal party with friends partaking of homemade cake, Ambrosia, Boiled Custard, and plenty of good strong coffee.

Helping out, always so much a part of life in Lynchburg, also expands during these weeks. For example, gifts to friends and neighbors almost always include homemade food, so that when the recipients host their parties, there will be plenty of good things on hand to serve. One woman mentioned that every year she bakes ten coconut cakes, five chocolate cakes, and several angel food cakes—all of which are warmly presented to friends to help them meet their entertaining needs.

The whole community cooperates when it comes to decorating the various churchs' Christmas trees. On the Sunday before the holiday, every member of each parish brings some treasured ornaments from home for the tree at his or her church. Each family also brings a covered dish; when the work is done, a fine potluck dinner is the reward for all.

Christmas is a time when just a little more care and preparation is put into everything, especially anything related to food and entertaining. And each hostess has her own favorite dishes which she serves year after year. These foods, anticipated by all guests, are just one more reflection of the appreciation for unchanging tradition felt by everyone in the town. Guests would be sorely disappointed, for example, if a particular hostess failed to serve her creamed sweet potatoes in hollowed-out orange shells. These attractive treats, topped with marshmallows and then browned in the oven, are so irresistible that most diners help themselves to at least two portions.

Another hostess makes a sort of pastry shell with an old-fashioned timbale iron. The iron is coated with a pancakelike batter and then plunged into hot oil. The resulting delicate, crisp shell is filled with creamed chicken for her guests' delight. Yet another hostess orders red and green loaves of bread from the bakery. These she alternately layers with tomato-cream cheese filling and chopped ham. The rainbow sandwiches are served with plates of cookies and candies when friends and neighbors drop by to express their holiday greetings.

In Lynchburg, as elsewhere, stockings filled with little treats are hung up for the children. And after the entire family opens their gifts they sit down to a big breakfast of country ham, biscuits, grits, scrambled eggs, and homemade sausages before going off to church. Christmas in Lynchburg is like Christmas in any other American small town, where people celebrate the pleasures of a tradition that has gone on for generations and will continue for generations to come. As one woman remarked, "Christmas always meant so much to everyone here, and it still does."

Miss Mary's kitchen, too, reflected the holiday spirit. This season was marked by an exciting array of especially tempting foods, and I've made a real effort to obtain as many of the recipes as possible so that you can recreate these splendid treats in your own kitchen for family and friends who visit during this festive season.

Some of Miss Mary's holiday recipes are unique versions of traditional Christmas foods everyone enjoys. Her Corn-Bread Dressing, for example, is enhanced with savory Giblet Gravy; Pumpkin Custard Pie is especially rich and creamy, and the Sweet Potatoes with Pecans are perked up with a dash of Jack Daniel's Whiskey. While liquor in any form was consumed at Miss Mary's only in the Boiled Custard or Eggnog especially prepared for holiday entertaining, several of her festive cooked recipes (such as sweet potatoes or cakes) were enlivened with just enough Jack Daniel's to let her guests know the meal was even more special than usual.

Among Mary Bobo's hundred-year-old recipes are foods you may never have sampled, but you'll find that they can lend a wonderful touch to your holiday parties. Scalloped Oysters are a perfect complement to roast turkey, as is Miss Mary's fruit-and nut-filled Cranberry Fluff. Fruitcake Cookies are superb treats to serve to guests who drop by, and they make delectable homemade gifts as well. For a grand finale to any holiday meal, try Fresh Coconut Cake. It was *always* served at Miss Mary's Christmas feast, and once you sample this rich, moist, snowy-white cake, it will certainly become a tradition in your home, too.

Chicory. If, when chicory first puts up shoots of new growth, the shoots have begun in total darkness, they make the finest salad available—one that would cost five dollars a pound in New York City even before our wild inflation achieved its present fantastic levels. The home grower may have this luxury, however, for nothing but his art and recreation as a horticulturist. Chicory salad is also a superior health food.

When the first shoots get sunlight and turn green, they are too bitter for salad; but if they are steeped (not boiled) they make a delicious, bitter green tea.

On Man and the Good Life. Leaves from the Notebook of Emmett Gowen.

Scalloped Oysters

❖

Of all the foods served with the holiday bird on Miss Mary's table, Scalloped Oysters were awaited with perhaps the most anticipation. The oysters are exceedingly rich, enveloped in a light, creamy breading. This dish is not unlike a dressing, and that's just how it's enjoyed—by the generous spoonful alongside slices of the bird.

In an inland town such as Lynchburg, it's often difficult to obtain fresh oysters. The canned variety may be substituted, with a slight loss in flavor and texture.

2 cups crumbs from saltine crackers	*Pepper*
1 pint fresh oysters, drained (reserve liquid)	*About 1 cup light cream or half and half*
	4 tablespoons butter

Grease an 8-inch-square baking dish and sprinkle half the cracker crumbs evenly in the bottom. Cover with half the oysters. Season with pepper. Add enough oyster liquid to the cream to make 2 cups liquid altogether (if there's less than 1 cup oyster liquid, use additional cream). Pour half of this mixture over the oysters and dot with half the butter. Repeat layers.

Bake the casserole in a 400° oven 20 minutes.

Yield: 6 servings.

Baked Hen with Corn-Bread Dressing and Giblet Gravy

❖

In Lynchburg, you're a lot more likely to be served a plump, juicy hen for the holiday meal than a turkey. The hen is cooked in a special way to keep it moist: first it's simmered until tender (the resulting broth goes into the dressing) and then it's baked in a hot oven until the skin is golden brown.

The dressing is a classic. To serve it in the traditional Southern fashion, spoon some Giblet Gravy over each portion.

Hen

1 6-pound hen	2 teaspoons salt
Water	Giblet Gravy (page 181)

Dressing

½ cup diced celery	1 teaspoon salt
1 small onion, chopped	½ teaspoon pepper
(about ½ cup)	½ teaspoon dried sage
2 tablespoons butter	2 eggs, beaten
3 cups corn-bread crumbs	1¾ cups warm broth from
2 cups white bread cubes	cooking hen

Place the hen in a large pot. Add enough water to just about cover it, then add the salt. Bring the liquid to a boil. Reduce the heat, cover, and simmer until the hen is tender, about 1 hour.

Remove the hen from the broth. Skim the fat from the broth and reserve 3¾ cups broth for the dressing and the Giblet Gravy. Place the hen on a greased baking sheet. Bake in a 400° oven 40 minutes, or until the skin is golden brown.

Meanwhile, in a small skillet, sauté the celery and onion in the butter until tender. Combine this mixture with all remaining dressing ingredients in a large bowl, and mix together gently but thoroughly.

Turn the dressing into a greased 1½-quart round casserole. Bake in a 400° oven during the last 30 minutes that the hen is baking.

Yield: 6 servings.

Note: You may use any type of corn-bread crumbs here. If you prepare Skillet Corn Bread (page 102), one half of that recipe will yield about three cups of crumbs.

Variation: Instead of turning the dressing into a casserole, it may be baked as individual "pones" and arranged on the platter to surround the holiday bird. To do this, shape the dressing, using cupped hands, into small, compact ovals and place on a greased baking sheet. Bake in a 400° oven about 10 minutes, or until crisp and browned.

Giblet Gravy

Giblets (gizzard and heart) and liver of hen	2 cups broth from cooking hen
Water	Salt, to taste
4 tablespoons butter	2 hard-cooked eggs, diced
¼ cup flour	

Place the giblets and liver in a saucepan and add enough water to cover amply. Bring the water to a boil and simmer, partially covered, until the giblets are tender, about 1 hour. Drain and finely chop (you will have to remove the rubbery outer membrane of the gizzard).

In a saucepan, melt the butter. Stir in the flour. Add the broth and cook, stirring constantly, until the mixture thickens and comes to a boil. Season with salt and stir in the giblets, liver, and eggs. Serve over portions of hen and dressing.

Sweet Potatoes with Pecans

❖

This festive sweet potato casserole is perked up with a liberal dash of Jack Daniel's—one of the few times that liquor in any form was used at Mary Bobo's. The pecans throughout and atop the casserole make this easily assembled dish a must on any holiday table.

4 large sweet potatoes or yams
* (see Note)*
½ stick (¼ cup) butter or
* margarine, softened*
¾ cup sugar

⅛ teaspoon salt
¼ cup Jack Daniel's Whiskey
½ cup pecans, coarsely
* chopped*

Place the sweet potatoes in a large saucepan and add enough water to cover completely. Bring the water to a boil, cover, and cook the potatoes until tender, about 35 minutes. Drain.

When the potatoes are cool enough to handle, peel off the skins. Place the potatoes in a mixing bowl and mash with the butter or margarine. Beat in the sugar, salt, and Jack Daniel's.

Spread half the potato mixture in a greased 1½-quart round casserole and sprinkle with half the pecans. Repeat layers.

Bake the casserole in a 325° oven until hot and the pecans turn light brown, about 30 minutes.

Yield: 6 to 8 servings.

Note: Yams make this casserole even richer.

Pineapple–Cheddar Casserole

❖

Here's a very special—and especially easy—side dish to accompany a Christmas ham. A layer of sweet, juicy pineapple slices is topped with melted Cheddar cheese and covered with buttery, toasted cracker crumbs.

1 20-ounce can pineapple chunks, preferably juice-packed
3 tablespoons flour
3 tablespoons sugar

1¼ cups shredded Cheddar cheese
1½ cups (about 25 to 30) crushed Ritz crackers
3 tablespoons butter, melted

Drain the pineapple, reserving 3 tablespoons juice. Arrange the pineapple on the bottom of a greased 1½-quart casserole.

Stir together the flour and sugar and sprinkle over the pineapple. Drizzle the reserved pineapple liquid over and top with the Cheddar cheese.

Mix together the crushed crackers and the melted butter and distribute over the cheese.

Bake the casserole, covered, in a 350° oven 15 minutes. Uncover and bake 10 minutes longer.

Yield: 6 to 8 servings.

Cranberry Fluff

❖

You'd have to look pretty hard to find a more festive version of cranberry sauce than this uncooked Cranberry Fluff that's chock-full of goodies like grapes, walnuts, marshmallows, fresh apples, and, of course, cranberries—all held together with freshly whipped cream. The Fluff was a must on Miss Mary's holiday table, and it was popular with everyone who ate at her house.

The cranberries must be very finely chopped or ground. You may use a manual grinder or a blender or food processor. The cranberries must be mixed with the sugar and marshmallows the night before you plan to serve the Fluff.

3 cups cranberries, finely chopped or ground
¾ cup sugar
3 cups miniature marshmallows
2 cups diced unpeeled apples
½ cup halved green seedless grapes

½ cup coarsely chopped walnuts or pecans
⅛ teaspoon salt
1 cup heavy (whipping) cream, whipped until stiff

In a large bowl, mix together the cranberries, sugar, and marshmallows. Cover and refrigerate overnight.

The next day, stir in the apples, grapes, walnuts or pecans, and salt. Chill until ready to serve.

Just before serving, fold in the whipped cream. Turn into a large serving bowl or spoon into individual lettuce-lined bowls.
Yield: 12 servings.

Jellied Cranberry–Orange Salad

❖

Here's another cranberry side dish that's a perfect accompaniment to your holiday turkey. This salad is less sweet and rich than Cranberry Fluff—the tart flavor of the oranges adds a complementary touch.

2 cups cranberries
2 whole oranges, seeded
3/4 cup sugar
1 cup chopped walnuts or
    pecans

1 8-ounce can crushed
    pineapple, drained
1 envelope plain gelatin
1 cup boiling water
1 cup cold water

Grind the cranberries and the oranges (including rind) in a food mill or food processor. Add the sugar, nuts, and pineapple. Stir well.

Dissolve the gelatin in the boiling water. Add the cold water and stir well. Add to the cranberry mixture.

Turn the contents of the bowl into a 1½-quart mold and chill until set. Serve on lettuce leaves, with a small garnish of mayonnaise on each portion.

Yield: 8 servings.

Boiled Custard

❖

This beverage—served as many serve eggnog throughout the holiday season—was a tradition at Miss Mary's and an especially welcome one because it was the only time an alcoholic beverage was offered to the guests. Actually, the custard itself contains no liquor, but at Miss Mary's (and at other homes in Lynchburg, and throughout the State of Tennessee for that matter), the custard was served with a small crystal pitcher of Jack Daniel's Whiskey, so guests could flavor it to taste.

For 6 servings

1 quart whole milk
3 egg yolks
½ cup plus 2 tablespoons
  sugar

Pinch salt
1 teaspoon vanilla extract

For 24 servings

1 gallon whole milk
12 egg yolks
2½ cups sugar

¼ teaspoon salt
4 teaspoons vanilla extract

Heat the milk in a saucepan until it just begins to simmer.

In a bowl, beat the egg yolks well with the sugar and salt. Gradually stir in some of the hot milk (about ¼ cup for 6 servings, 1 cup for 24 servings). This will reduce the chances of the egg yolks' curdling.

Pour the egg mixture into the pan of milk. Cook over low direct heat or in the top of a double boiler until the mixture thickens enough to coat the back of a wooden spoon. Stir constantly as it cooks, and if you are cooking over a direct flame, don't let it boil.

Let the custard cool. Stir in the vanilla and chill until ready to serve.

Serve in cups or glasses, topped with a scoop of whipped cream or vanilla ice cream and a pitcher of Jack Daniel's Whiskey passed on the side.

Yield: 6 or 24 servings.

Note: Actually, the word "boiled" is something of a misnomer because the last thing you'd want to do with custard is boil it, for this will cause the eggs to curdle. "Boiled" refers to the fact that it's cooked on top of the stove, as opposed to a baked custard that's cooked in the oven. Boiled custards are generally creamier in texture, without that baked-on skin on top. If you've never made a custard before, you may wish to use a double boiler because this almost completely eliminates any chance of curdling. But if you're careful, you can use an ordinary saucepan, in which case the mixture will cook far more quickly.

I have given two sets of proportions for the custard, one that produces 6 servings, the other making enough for an open house for 24 guests.

April 7. Luther N. came with Sion to see some fine pigs. They concluded to have some fun shooting. Mrs. Hattie was going to shoot, too. It was amusing beyond description to watch Luther shoot the first time. His target was the big plum tree in full bloom. He afterwards killed a sparrow and was the proudest boy in town, but he acknowledged it was an accident. Tonight all of the N. family, including Mrs. Mollie N., came over and stayed until bedtime. Mrs. Hattie N. made us some sweet music on the organ and guitar. She plays beautifully. We all spent an enjoyable occasion and I hope it will soon be repeated, for I dearly love good music and the friendship of my neighbors.

Sue Dance Record's Diary, 1896.

Tennessee Eggnog

❖

While Boiled Custard was traditionally served at Miss Mary's during the holiday season, when Ervin Crutcher was still alive (he was the husband of Mary Bobo's daughter, Louise), he contributed this rich beverage to the festivities each year.

6 eggs, separated
1½ cups sugar, divided
1½ cups Jack Daniel's
  Whiskey

1 pint heavy (whipping)
  cream
1 cup milk
Grated nutmeg

Beat the egg whites until stiff. Gradually beat in ½ cup sugar. The mixture should be thick and glossy. Set aside.

In another bowl, beat the egg yolks. Gradually beat in ½ cup sugar. Beat in the Jack Daniel's Whiskey.

In a third bowl, beat the heavy cream until stiff. Beat in the remaining ½ cup sugar.

Place the egg white mixture in a punch bowl. Fold in the egg yolk mixture, then the whipped cream, and finally the milk. Stir well. Serve very cold, with a sprinkling of nutmeg on each portion.

Yield: about 10 cups, serving 16 guests.

Fresh Coconut Cake

❖

This spectacular four-layer cake is made each year for Christmas dinner. It is a magnificent, high white cake that's sprinkled with the liquid from the coconut and then put together with a soft white "divinity" icing (so-called because it's made just like the candy, only cooked to a lower temperature). The cake is then liberally covered with shredded fresh coconut, a truly fitting end to any feast.

Cake

1 fresh coconut
2 sticks (1 cup) butter,
  softened
2 cups granulated sugar
8 egg whites
1 teaspoon vanilla extract

¼ teaspoon almond extract
1 cup milk, divided
3¼ cups flour
4 teaspoons baking powder
¼ teaspoon salt
⅓ cup confectioners' sugar

Icing

2 egg whites
2 cups sugar
2 tablespoons light corn syrup

⅔ cup water
2 teaspoons vanilla extract
½ teaspoon almond extract

Prepare the coconut according to the instructions on page 196. Reserve ¼ cup liquid from the coconut for moistening the cake. You should have about 3 cups shredded coconut.

To make the cake, cream the butter with the granulated sugar in a large bowl. Beat in the egg whites, then the extracts. Add half the milk and beat well.

In another bowl, stir together the flour, baking powder, and salt. Beat into the creamed mixture, along with the remaining milk.

Divide the batter between 2 greased and floured 9-inch layer cake pans. Bake the layers in a 350° oven until a toothpick inserted in the center comes out clean, about 45 minutes. Transfer to a rack to cool. When completely cooled, split each layer in half horizontally. Mix together the reserved coconut liquid and the confectioners' sugar and sprinkle evenly over the tops of each of the four layers.

Prepare the icing. In a mixing bowl, beat the egg whites until stiff.

In a medium saucepan, bring the sugar, corn syrup, and water to a boil, stirring until the sugar dissolves. Cover the pan and cook until the mixture comes to a full, rolling boil. Remove from the heat.

While beating, gradually add ⅓ cup of the hot syrup to the egg whites. Return the pan to the heat and continue boiling, without stirring, until the temperature reaches 238° to 240° on a candy thermometer. While beating at high speed, gradually beat the hot syrup into the egg whites. Beat in the extracts and then continue beating until the icing is of spreading consistency, about 5 minutes longer.

Assemble the cake by spreading a small amount of icing between layers and sprinkling about ¼ of the coconut over each layer of icing. Spread the remaining icing over the top and sides of the cake and sprinkle with the remaining coconut. Let the icing set for at least 10 minutes before cutting the cake.

Yield: 20 to 24 servings.

Note: This cake calls for nearly a dozen egg whites. The yolks may be used in Eggnog (page 189) or Boiled Custard (page 186).

Christmas Fruitcake

❖

Anyone lucky enough to drop by Miss Mary's during the holiday season was likely to be served a thin slice of her exceptionally rich and delicious fruitcake. The cake contains all the traditional ingredients—candied cherries, orange peel, dried fruits, and nuts —plus a few that make it extra-special: dark cocoa, grape jelly, and flavorful blackberry cordial.

2/3 cup butter or margarine, softened
2/3 cup sugar
4 eggs
1/3 cup grape jelly
1/3 cup blackberry cordial
1 1/3 cups flour, divided
1 1/2 tablespoons cocoa, sifted if lumpy
1/2 teaspoon cinnamon
1/2 teaspoon nutmeg
3/4 cup raisins
1 cup chopped dates
3/4 cup figs, diced
2/3 cup candied orange peel, diced
2/3 cup candied cherries, halved
2/3 cup candied pineapple, diced
1 cup slivered blanched almonds
1 cup coarsely chopped pecans

In a large bowl, beat the butter or margarine with the sugar. Beat in the eggs, then the jelly and cordial.

In another bowl, stir together 1 cup flour with the cocoa, cinnamon, and nutmeg.

In a third bowl, toss all fruits and nuts with the remaining 1/3 cup flour.

Beat the dry ingredients into the liquid mixture and then stir in the fruits and nuts until well mixed in.

Pack the batter firmly into a well-greased and floured 9 by

5-inch loaf pan. Bake the cake in a 250° oven 5 hours, or until a toothpick inserted in the center comes out clean. Let cool thoroughly before slicing.

Mary Bobo recommended wrapping this cake in foil to age for a month before eating. While this does improve the flavor, if you're in a hurry to try your cake, this mellowing isn't necessary.

Yield: 1 loaf (about 20 servings).

Note: This recipe makes one loaf (approximately 4 pounds), but it can easily be doubled or tripled if you'd like to keep one for yourself and give others as gifts.

February 6. Mr. R. has been very busy all day in court. Haden and Ila took dinner with us; and although we were not expecting company, we had plenty and they seemed to enjoy their dinner. Eula has been busy this evening dressing dolls for the little girl. Mary and I spent the evening with Mrs. John N., Mrs. B. and Mrs. Mollie N. piecing quilts and embroidery together. A little fun kept us all busy— we did not talk about our neighbors as women are said to do, but we had a good time.

Sue Dance Record's Diary, 1896.

Tennessee Whiskey Cake

❖

Here's another fruitcake, this one without the customary candied cherries and other fruits. Instead, it's simply loaded with raisins and pecans and has a fine, spirited flavor.

6 eggs, separated
2 sticks (1 cup) butter,
  softened
2 cups sugar
½ cup Jack Daniel's Whiskey
2 cups browned flour (see
  Note below)

½ teaspoon nutmeg,
  preferably freshly grated
1 15-ounce box raisins
  (2½ cups)
6 ounces coarsely chopped
  pecans (1½ cups)

In a bowl, beat the egg whites until stiff. Set aside.

In a large bowl, cream the butter with the sugar. Beat in the egg yolks, then the whiskey.

In another bowl, stir together the flour and nutmeg. Beat into the creamed ingredients. Fold in the egg whites, raisins, and pecans.

Turn the batter into a greased and floured 9-inch tube pan. Bake the cake in a 300° oven about 2¼ hours, or until a toothpick inserted in the center comes out clean. Let cool thoroughly before slicing.

Yield: 16 servings.

Note: This recipe calls for the flour to be browned, a procedure that lends an extra-dark color and slightly nutty taste to the cake. To brown flour, place it in a dry skillet and cook, stirring, over medium heat until it is pale brown in color.

Pumpkin Custard Pie

❖

A traditional holiday recipe at Miss Mary's, as in the rest of the country, this is the classic baked pumpkin pie, with a rich egg custard base and plenty of spices to perk it up.

Recipe for 1-crust pastry
  (page 115)
1½ cups mashed pumpkin
  (see Note below)
¾ cup sugar
1½ teaspoons cinnamon
1 teaspoon ground ginger
½ teaspoon nutmeg

½ teaspoon ground cloves
¼ teaspoon salt
3 eggs
⅔ cup evaporated milk
⅔ cup milk
1 cup heavy (whipping)
  cream, whipped until stiff
  with 2 tablespoons sugar

Roll out the pastry dough to an 11-inch circle and fit into a deep 9-inch pie plate.

In a large mixing bowl, stir together the pumpkin, sugar, spices, and salt. Beat in the eggs and then stir in the evaporated and regular milk. Pour into the pastry.

Bake the pie in a 400° oven about 1 hour, or until it is set and browned. Let cool on a rack.

When serving, garnish each slice with freshly whipped cream.
Yield: 8 servings.

Note: You may use canned solid-pack pumpkin (not pumpkin pie filling) or freshly cooked pumpkin in this recipe. To cook fresh pumpkin, wash it, cut it in half, and remove the seeds. Place, cut side down, on a baking sheet and add ½ inch water. Bake in a 350° oven about 1 hour or until tender. Scrape out the pulp and put through a ricer or strainer.

Ambrosia

❖

Ambrosia, defined in the dictionary as food for the gods, is a classic Southern dessert that combines pineapple, oranges, and coconut in a refreshing compote that's perfect after a heavy holiday meal. The dessert evolved because so many people were given crates of oranges and fresh coconuts during the holidays. Even today, no Southern cook would ever make Ambrosia with anything less than freshly grated coconut, and at Miss Mary's, the dessert was served with slices of her Fresh Coconut Cake (page 190).

5 large oranges, peeled and sectioned
2 bananas, sliced
1 cup coarsely grated fresh coconut (see Note below)

1 16-ounce can juice-packed chunk pineapple, undrained
¼ cup sugar, or to taste

Mix all ingredients well and chill until ready to serve (preferably, and traditionally, in crystal bowls).

Yield: 6 to 8 servings.

Note: To prepare fresh coconut, pierce the three eyes of the coconut with an ice pick or skewer and drain the liquid. Bake the coconut in a 400° oven 15 minutes; this causes the hard shell to crack. Split the coconut in half and pry the meat from the shell with the point of a sharp knife, With a vegetable peeler, remove the brown membrane. Cut the coconut meat into small pieces and grate on a hand grater or in a food processor. The grated coconut meat will keep well, stored in the refrigerator in a covered container, for several weeks. One coconut will yield about 3 cups of shredded coconut meat.

Fruitcake Cookies

❖

These luscious morsels are made each year during the holiday season and served on small plates, accompanied by squares of rich fudge. The cookies are big and chewy, almost like old-fashioned hermits—with plenty of spices, dates, candied fruits, and pecans. They keep well and are perfect for holiday gifts.

1 stick (½ cup) butter,
  softened
¾ cup plus 2 tablespoons
  sugar
2 eggs
2 tablespoons Jack Daniel's
  Whiskey
2½ tablespoons water
¼ teaspoon baking soda
1½ cups flour
1½ teaspoons cinnamon

1 teaspoon nutmeg
¼ teaspoon salt
1 pound dates, chopped
  (about 3 cups)
4 ounces candied pineapple,
  chopped (about ⅔ cup)
8 ounces mixed red and green
  candied cherries, halved
  (about 1 cup)
8 ounces pecans, chopped
  (about 1¼ cups)

In a large bowl, cream the butter with the sugar. Beat in the eggs, then the whiskey. Stir together the water and baking soda and beat in.

In another bowl, stir together the flour, cinnamon, nutmeg, and salt. Beat into the creamed mixture. Stir in all fruits and nuts. The batter will be very stiff.

Drop the batter by rounded tablespoonfuls onto greased baking sheets. Bake the cookies in a 350° oven about 20 minutes. The tops will still be slightly soft and the undersides will be lightly browned. Transfer to a rack to cool. Store in an airtight container.

Yield: about 50 cookies.

January 22. Quite a heavy rain fell this morning. I went to town shopping after dinner and when I returned found that Cousin Timmie M. had come to make a short visit and show one the way to her house. Oh, my life is so full of duties that I have no time, it seems, to make visits for pleasure's sake. I often wish I did. But by the time I attend to all my church meetings, etc. in that line, visit the sick and go where I feel duty demands, I have very little time for visits of pleasure only. In fact, I can't do the half I want to do and that needs to be done. Prayer meeting tonight was very interesting. The 12th Chap. of Heb. was the lesson read and comments on the life of Paul being the chief subject.

Sue Dance Record's Diary, 1896.

Pecan Fudge

❖

This recipe belongs to Miss Mary's daughter, Louise Crutcher, who greeted guests at the noon meal every day. Louise served this rich, nut-filled fudge each year during the holiday season, accompanied by Fruitcake Cookies (page 197).

3 cups sugar
¼ cup unsweetened cocoa
1 stick (½ cup) butter, plus
   butter for pan

1 cup evaporated milk
1 teaspoon vanilla extract
1 cup coarsely chopped pecans

In a large heavy saucepan, place the sugar, cocoa, butter, and milk. Cook over moderately high heat, stirring, until the butter melts. Continue to cook at a slow boil, not stirring at all, until the temperature reaches 234° on a candy thermometer (the soft-ball stage). Remove from the heat.

Let the fudge sit undisturbed until it cools to 110° (comfortably warm). Add the vanilla and pecans. With a wooden spoon, beat the fudge until it is very thick. It will lose its shine and turn a lighter shade of brown.

Butter an 8-inch-square pan and quickly pour in the fudge. Let sit 10 minutes and then cut into 36 squares. Let sit until firm.

Yield: about 2 pounds.

Note: If you lack a candy thermometer, you can judge when the mixture has reached the soft-ball stage by dropping a small amount (equivalent to about ⅛ teaspoon) into a glass of cold water. Pick up the piece of candy. If it holds together and has a chewy texture, it is ready.

Tennessee Whiskey Surprise Balls

❖

These chocolate-coated confections are sweet and rich, with creamy centers that hold a pecan crunch. At Miss Mary's the candies were served during the holiday season, and they make wonderful Christmas gifts as well.

Although they certainly *taste* as delicious as anything you can buy anywhere, it's difficult to make chocolate-coated candies that look perfect unless you have professional equipment. One solution often utilized by Southern cooks is to add some paraffin (Gulf Wax) to the chocolate when melting it; the wax helps the chocolate stay smooth and enhances its dipping qualities.

1 stick (½ cup) butter,
  softened
1 1-pound box confectioners'
  sugar
¼ cup Jack Daniel's Whiskey

About 30 pecan halves
3 6-ounce packages semisweet
  chocolate morsels
⅓ bar paraffin (Gulf Wax)

Cream the butter and sugar until smooth. Beat in the whiskey.

Shape the mixture into balls about 1½ inches in diameter, putting a pecan half in the center of each. The easiest way to do this is to scoop up the correct amount of filling with a teaspoon, insert the pecan into the center of the filling, and then push the filling off the spoon with your finger, as you would the batter for drop cookies. Refrigerate the balls in a single layer on a plate for at least 1 hour.

Melt the chocolate and paraffin in the top of a double boiler. Dip the balls, one at a time, into the chocolate and place on a

plate or piece of waxed paper. The easiest way to do this is to
drop the ball into the chocolate and rotate it with a teaspoon
until coated; then scoop it out with the spoon.

Let the balls sit in the refrigerator until set. The candies should
be served at room temperature, but store them in the refrigerator
(or freezer for longer storage).

Yield: about 30 candies.

Recipe Index